Welcome to East Hampton:

We cordially invite you to share
our favorite local recipes and
famous ambience

SAMPLE A SYBARITE'S BREAKFAST
- Peaches in Champagne
- Croissants Stuffed with Prosciutto
- Café au Lait

INDULGE IN AN EAST END LUNCH
- Greta Garbo's Cream of Tomato Soup
- Eastern Long Island Clam Pie
- Coleslaw
- Beach Plum Pudding

ENJOY AN OUTDOOR DINNER
- Barbecued Chicken
- Baked Summer Squash Casserole
- Herbed Garlic Bread
- Sliced Tomatoes Vinaigrette
- Strawberries and Peaches in Cointreau

MAGNIFICENT EATING ALL DAY LONG
FROM ONE OF THE FINEST COOKBOOKS
EVER WRITTEN

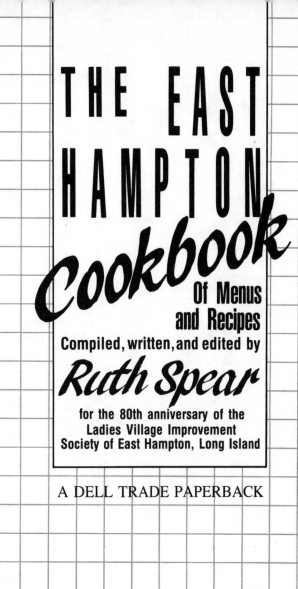

THE EAST HAMPTON

Cookbook

Of Menus and Recipes

Compiled, written, and edited by

Ruth Spear

for the 80th anniversary of the
Ladies Village Improvement
Society of East Hampton, Long Island

A DELL TRADE PAPERBACK

Published by
Dell Publishing
a division of
The Bantam Doubleday Dell Publishing Group, Inc.
1 Dag Hammarskjold Plaza
New York, New York 10017

Dell ® TM 681510, Dell Publishing, a division of the Bantam Doubleday Dell Publishing Group, Inc.

ISBN: 0-440-50014-1

Designed by Sheree L. Goodman

Printed in the United States of America

June 1988

10 9 8 7 6 5 4 3 2 1
MV

To Jeanette Edwards Rattray, a great lady,
who cherished East Hampton's past
with feet firmly planted in the present
and eyes on the future.

Acknowledgments

The preparation of this book was aided and enhanced by many people. June Kelly, LVIS president from 1971 to 1974, first enthusiastically embraced the concept of the new cookbook and was a great source of moral support throughout the year and a half it took to compile and refine it, as was Ann Jones Light. Florence Fabricant was generous with her time and ideas, read text, and made suggestions; so did Reva Wurtzburger, who was always available to discuss menus, test recipes, and work out problems. Helen Duncan and a crew of friends also tasted recipes and tackled the formidable job of indexing with great zeal and dedication. My deepest gratitude goes to Harvey Spear, who daily braved the threat of high cholesterol and corpulence to taste and retaste, and to the over seventy LVIS members and friends (their names appear at the end of the book) who contributed favorite recipes and ideas.

R.S.

Contents

*indicates dishes that travel well

*indicates dishes that travel well

Foreword

It is a source of special pleasure, if not to say gratification, to know that I live in a community where conceivably there are more fine and talented cooks than any other community in America. It is not surprising, therefore, that there are several recipes of uncommon excellence reflected in this book. And I am amused that some of them have a distinct flavor of the region, although they were created not by native Bonackers, but by people who moved here, some of them late in life.

One who comes to mind is Nora Bennett, for many years the devoted cook of a good friend of mine. He invited me over one day to sample Nora's famous clam chowder. It was devastatingly good. She was very proud of the recipe and had sworn never to give it to a soul; nevertheless she kindly invited me to come into her kitchen and watch. I measured all of her ingredients while she sat and ground up the celery, clams, and so on, the grinder attached to an old chair bottom. Although Nora was born in County Galway, she gave a special meaning to East Hampton clam chowder.

It is not simply a love of East Hampton and an overwhelming admiration for the good works of the Ladies Village Improvement Society that impels me to say that this is, to my taste, an outstanding cookbook. The recipes have been selected with unerring taste and discrimination and they have been edited painstakingly with a very special enthusiasm and awareness of what makes a recipe work.

Craig Claiborne
East Hampton, N.Y.

Introduction

In 1898, a slim volume of local East Hampton "receipts" appeared, published by the newly formed Ladies Village Improvement Society for the purpose of raising funds to aid them in their work. Every decade or so, a new collection was gotten together, each a little larger than before. They enjoyed great popularity and some of the older ones are now considered collector's items. This, the eleventh, is a radical departure from its predecessors. First it reflects food as a life-style rather than only food indigenous to the area. Secondly, it is a menu cookbook. For why we eat what we do, and how, and when, is no longer based only on local custom and availability (although that certainly plays a part). Our large artists' community, an ever-growing group of second-home owners and their guests of widely divergent ethnic and national backgrounds, with palates honed by travel, have made once exotic dishes like ratatouille and moussaka as common fare as East End clam pie.

The second home, now likely to be kept open most of the year and servantless all of it, comes to life on the weekend and demands meal planning of a high order. The family piles out of the car hungry and has to be fed. There is precious little time for shopping and cooking; one wants something a bit festive and special. Houseguests, a firmly entrenched custom, complicate the picture further. Thoughts about food for the weekend often begin on Wednesday; thinking in terms of whole menus can expedite planning and shopping. So can working around dishes that can be prepared largely ahead with relatively little fuss, using seasonally available ingredients.

The menus and recipes in this book have been gathered with that, as well as the overall country life-style, in mind. The food is, for the most part, hearty and simple, though not necessarily easy. Convenience foods appear rarely. We are extremely fortunate to have still available the superb seafood, vegetables, and fruit for which the area is famous, so these appear frequently in our menus, which explains our being slightly heavy in dishes involving clams, corn, squash, strawberries, beach plums, and the like.

The menus themselves are not meant to be rigid prescriptions—rather they are takeoff points—suggestions for felicitous combinations that you may use in whole or part—or prepare ahead—or consume on the spot. Make a family meal out of a company menu by leaving off the first course, or broaden the scope of a simple one by adding to it. Fresh fruit, perhaps with a bit of cheese, is always a nice way to wind up a meal if there's no time or inclination to make dessert. A good fresh crusty Italian loaf and some wine can elevate the simplest of meals.

Whether your life involves a second home or you merely care about food and feeding those you care about, we hope you will be inspired by this collection.

Ruth Spear
East Hampton, N.Y.

The LVIS: A Brief History

The current nostalgia for the good old days would have brought forth derisive comments from the handful of East Hampton women who founded the Ladies Village Improvement Society ninety years ago, when roads were unpaved and unlighted and there were no sidewalks or bicycle paths. Even then, the ladies complained that the charm of East Hampton was beginning to fade. In 1895, a notice appeared in the East Hampton *Star,* summoning ''All ladies interested in a Ladies Improvement Society to meet in the annex of Clinton Hall on Monday evening at 7 P.M.'' The notice was printed along with an editorial comment: ''Good! We trust the ladies will go ahead and begin the grand work of improving.'' At once the ladies began their ''grand work.'' Three weeks later they held the first of innumerable fund-raising events, a New England supper on New Year's Eve, 1895. This affair brought seventy-five dollars into their treasury, and by the end of the month the new society had thirty charter members. They decided that theirs was to be no ''pink tea organization,'' and gave notice that their objectives would include ''the improvement of the highways, sidewalks, cemeteries and any other work for the general interest and welfare of the village.''

The first actual ''improvement'' work for the village was accomplished by the ladies themselves. Tucking up their long skirts and grabbing shovels, they dug and set out over one hundred honeysuckle plants around the fences of the two cemeteries. They planted grass on the new and unsightly railroad banks, persuaded Mr. Jeremiah Huntting to plant vines on his lumber yard sheds, and set about beautifying the railroad station with Virginia creeper. By the end of their first summer, the LVIS had raised an even thousand dollars through subscriptions, a fair and sociables. With this money, the first improvement to the Main Street in the village in two and a half centuries was accomplished. The women purchased lamps and wooden posts, bought oil and hired a lamplighter. *Their* Main Street was to be well lighted at night.

Other projects followed at a relentless pace. Bicycle paths for the cycle enthusiasts were built to keep the "wheels" out of the streets and off the sidewalks. A year later, when the treasury permitted, $600 was paid for two sprinkling carts and a contract awarded to a driver and his team to water down the dusty streets.

The ladies finally got into the road building business in September 1899. A committee traveled up and down Long Island—Jamaica, Far Rockaway, Patchogue—talking to road engineers. Finally, by January 1900, the first portion of Main Street, from Newtown Lane to Huntting Lane, had been paved, complete with cobblestone gutters. Eventually, Main Street's hard durable surface went all the way to the Main Beach.

It was once stated at a meeting that the "early LVIS took care of the fundamentals so that the present society can devote its attention to the trimmings." These trimmings referred, of course, to the care of the trees, the village greens, Town Pond, and other projects as they came along. If "better roads" was the battle cry of the first two decades of the society, "no signs," was the next. East Hampton became a "signless town" during the 1920s, which gained nation-wide attention for the LVIS. In 1964, the ladies talked village officials into an ordinance limiting their use.

The greatest challenge the ladies faced came in 1938 when the century's worst hurricane struck East Hampton. In one unforgettable afternoon, great elms that had shaded Main Street for a hundred years were uprooted; the destruction in other parts of the village was indescribable. Barely had the winds subsided when the LVIS tree committee, headed by Mrs. William A. Lockwood, began rolling up its sleeves. Working with village officials, they grimly set about clearing away the debris and took the lead in replanting the village streets. With similar determination, the women have grappled with Dutch elm disease since the 1950s and carry on a continuing program to save the elms. The losses are replaced with trees of other varieties.

Since World War II, the LVIS has faced the problems of enormous and unexpected growth and development in East Hampton. In refus-ing to turn their backs on the inevitable, the ladies have worked to keep the charm of the village intact through the enactment of zoning ordinances, and over the past ten years, unlimited amounts of time have been devoted to development planning and the preservation of landmarks and open spaces.

Following that first supper in 1895, the ladies had announced that their next project would be a cookbook, containing "receipts" of the best cooks in the village, to be sold at a fair the following summer. The fair and the cookbook ideas have continued, netting the thousands of dollars needed to accomplish the improvement and maintenance the society has undertaken.

Their eleventh cookbook contains an approach to cooking that is a far cry from the first edition in 1898 entitled *The Way We Cook in East Hampton*. Few cooks today could or would use a receipt for canaille bread ("take wheat bread sponge, mix canaille [corn meal] enough so the spoon will stand upright in the mixture") or scrap cake ("a half pound of lard scraps chopped fine") or superior sponge cake ("1¼ lbs sugar beat to a froth with the yolks of 12 eggs"). Yet, the new book could be subtitled *The Way We Cook in East Hampton Today*.

Apart from cookbook sales, it is the fair that has given most of the income. The first one in 1896 in Clinton Academy was most modest, but the essentials were there: booths and persuasive young matrons selling cakes, candies, aprons and needlework. When the fairs outgrew Clinton Hall, they were moved onto the Village Green, where they remained for most of the next forty years. But the wear and tear on the grass finally proved too much. Traditionally held on the last Friday of July, the fair is today spread out on the Mulford House grounds.

Residents take the LVIS for granted, something that has always been here, like Town Pond. Yet when a newcomer asks in a puzzled way, "Just what is this LVIS?" it is difficult to come up with a quick answer. It *is* a group of over four hundred women who are interested in the welfare of the village. It *is* a group of women who have a fair every summer, a Bargain Box shop on Main Street and a Bargain Books on Newtown Lane. It *is* a group of women who offer major scholarships and contribute to local institutions. But it is so much more. Where the ladies have led, the village and town officials have followed. Their efforts have resulted in a place called by many "the most beautiful village in America." When any newcomer wonders how this came about, we like to give the same answer a young gas station attendant gave an inquirer. He said, with pride, "The ladies did it."

—Averill Geus

EAST
Breakfasts & Brunches
HAMPTON

A HEARTY BREAKFAST

Fresh fruit salad

Sunnyside-up eggs

*Fried tomato halves

*Home-fried potatoes

Country sausage

*Buttered baking
powder biscuits

Coffee

Fried tomato halves

Prepare tomato halves as described in the recipe for baked eggs and tomatoes (see Index) and fry them, but do not bake. Use to garnish breakfast eggs.

Home-fried potatoes

1   medium boiled potato, peeled, per person
1   tablespoon butter for each
1   tablespoon vegetable oil for each
    Salt and freshly ground pepper

Cut potatoes into ¼-inch slices. Dry slices and sauté in equal parts of butter and oil in a heavy skillet. Cook slowly, turning from time to time, until crisp and golden brown. Season before serving.

Buttered baking powder biscuits

1	cup sifted all-purpose flour
2	tablespoons sugar
1½	teaspoons baking powder
½	teaspoon salt
⅓	cup melted butter or margarine
3	tablespoons milk
1	egg

Preheat oven to 350°.

Sift dry ingredients together into a bowl. Mix shortening, milk, and egg, and stir in dry ingredients with a fork. Drop a teaspoon of the mixture into ungreased muffin tins and bake for 25 minutes or until lightly browned. Makes 12 biscuits.

Peaches in champagne

6	ripe peaches
2	tablespoons lemon juice
⅓	cup sugar
½	bottle champagne, chilled (12 ounces)

Put peaches in boiling water for a few seconds to loosen skin. Peel. Slice lengthwise in thin slices. Add sugar and lemon juice, mix well and chill in refrigerator for an hour or so. Arrange slices in large chilled goblets or wide champagne glasses and pour 2 ounces champagne over each. Serves 6.

Croissants stuffed with prosciutto

Heat good-quality frozen croissants or buy them from a French baker. (They keep wonderfully in the freezer and are a lovely way to pamper weekend guests.) Split the warmed croissants lengthwise and insert a rolled-up slice of prosciutto ham in each. Serve with freshly brewed strong coffee (preferably made by some filter method and not perked) and a pot of hot milk.

Brie with homemade strawberry preserves

A ripe Brie, possibly left over from dinner the night before, makes an unusual and satisfying breakfast spread accompanied by homemade strawberry preserves (see Index) and an assortment of breads and rolls.

Cinnamon cheese toast

Heap ricotta cheese on a slice of whole wheat or regular toast and sprinkle with cinnamon sugar. Serves one.

BREAKFAST ANY TIME OF THE YEAR

Fresh orange juice

Toasted English muffins, toasted French bread

*Brie with homemade strawberry preserves

Café au lait

QUICK BREAKFAST

Fresh-squeezed grapefruit juice

*Cinnamon cheese toast

Coffee or tea

Compote of strawberries and melon balls

1   pint strawberries, hulled
1   cantaloupe
1   honeydew or Cranshaw melon
     Sugar to taste
     Lemon juice
     Mint for garnish (optional)

Make melon balls using a ball cutter. Mix fruits, stir sugar into lemon juice and pour over. Chill for ½ hour before serving. Garnish with mint leaves if desired.

Corn pancakes

¾   cup all-purpose flour
1   tablespoon baking powder
1   teaspoon salt
½   teaspoon freshly ground pepper
1   egg
1   10½-ounce can creamed corn
     Butter for skillet

Mix flour, baking powder, salt, pepper, and egg. Add corn and mix well. Brush a skillet with butter and drop mixture on by tablespoons, a few at a time. Cook until undersides are golden, then turn with a spatula and cook other side. Keep warm in oven, lightly covered, until all are cooked. Serves 4.

SUMMER
BREAKFAST I

*Compote of
strawberries and
melon balls

*Corn pancakes

*Oven-baked bacon

Coffee

Oven-baked bacon

Preheat oven to 350°. Lay bacon slices on a flat rimmed baking sheet and bake 14–20 minutes, until bacon is crisp and cooked through. Drain on paper. Bacon cooked this way shrinks less than when cooked in a pan and does not curl or get frizzled. Any thickness can be used; simply adjust the cooking time accordingly. Bacon cut thick from the slab, rind removed, is particularly delicious when oven-baked.

Bacon can also be cooked in advance by this method, particularly advantageous when a large quantity is needed. Do it the night before or whenever you are using the oven. Do not allow to cook through completely. Drain, wrap, and refrigerate. In the morning, preheat the oven and finish baking to desired degree of doneness while you prepare the rest of the breakfast.

Baked eggs and tomatoes

SUMMER BREAKFAST II

Blueberries with brown sugar and cream

*Baked eggs and tomatoes

Toasted English muffins

Coffee

1   tomato per person
2   eggs per person
    Salt, freshly ground pepper
    Slivered garlic
    Chopped parsley
    Olive oil

Preheat oven to 400°.

Cut tomatoes in half. Seed the halves carefully with the tip of a pointed knife. Season with salt and pepper and parsley and push some garlic slivers into the tomatoes.

Heat the oil in a skillet and fry the tomato halves gently, cut side down.

Have ready an ovenproof dish large enough to hold all the eggs and tomatoes or a porcelain ramekin for each person. Remove tomato halves carefully from skillet and place them fried side up in the dish or dishes. Spoon the frying oil from the skillet into the bottom of the dish. Break an egg over each tomato. Bake at 400° until the eggs are set (the whites opaque but the yolks still runny). Salt the eggs at the last minute before serving.

Kedgeree

Approximately 1 pound fresh cooked fish (such as bass, salmon, weakfish, or cod).

Some liquid reserved from cooking the fish, or if there is none, chicken broth.

2	teaspoons salt
3	to 4 cups cooked rice
2	tablespoons butter, melted
2	eggs, boiled 6 minutes
2	tablespoons minced onions
	Salt, freshly ground black pepper
	Cayenne pepper
½	teaspoon curry powder
2	tablespoons chopped parsley
	Tomato and cucumber slices
1	egg, hard-cooked and quartered

Mix fish with rice and melted butter.

Shell the eggs and chop fine (they will be a bit runny). Stir into the rice mixture, add onion, and season with salt, several good grindings of pepper and dash of cayenne, and curry. Moisten with some fish liquid or chicken broth. The mixture should be moist enough to hold together, but not soggy or swimming.

The mixture is then ready to be turned out onto a serving dish and molded into a cake with the back of a fork, or it can be packed lightly into a buttered 2-quart ring mold, and turned out. Garnish with parsley and decorate plate with tomato and cucumber slices and egg quarters. Serves 4.

SPRING OR SUMMER BRUNCH

*Kedgeree

Melba rye toast

*Raw spinach and mushroom salad

*Strawberry tarts

Raw spinach and mushroom salad

Juice of ½ lemon
¼   cup soy sauce
2   teaspoons sugar
2   tablespoons peanut oil
¼   cup sesame seeds
1½   pounds fresh spinach, washed, dried, stems removed
½   pound raw mushrooms, sliced

Mix lemon juice, soy sauce, sugar, and oil in a small saucepan and stir over gentle heat until sugar dissolves. Let cool. Toast sesame seeds in a dry frying pan over medium heat until they color and start to pop. Crush seeds between two pieces of waxed paper with a rolling pin and stir them into cooled sauce. Pour over spinach and mushrooms in a large bowl and toss very well. Serves 6–8.

Strawberry tarts

1   cup red currant jelly
2   tablespoons sugar
1   tablespoon hot water
1   tablespoon Cointreau or Cognac
6   pâté brisée shells, baked (see Index)
2–3   pints unblemished medium-size strawberries

Put jelly, sugar, and water in a small saucepan and heat gently until a froth appears and jelly thickens. Stir occasionally and do not let it burn around edges. Remove from heat and cool slightly. With a pastry brush or the back of a spoon, paint a thin coat of glaze over the bottom of the cooled pastry shells. (This will help keep berries from making shells soggy.) Let dry 5 minutes.

Prepare berries: Wash briefly and dry well on paper towels. Remove stems with the tip of a sharp knife. Try not to cut into berries as this will cause them to "bleed" juice into the pastry. Stand berries upright shoulder to shoulder in shells. Spoon or paint glaze over berries, reheating glaze gently as necessary if it hardens. Serves 6.

Note: Although shells and berries can be prepared ahead, tarts should be assembled as near to serving time as possible—say an hour or two beforehand.

Cheese soufflé

Many otherwise fearless cooks are intimidated by soufflés; actually, it is hard to have a failure if the egg whites are well and properly beaten and you avoid opening the oven door during the first 20 minutes of baking. The procedure can seem tricky, however, if you do not (1) take the time to make all the preparations at the beginning and (2) start out using the proper-size saucepan and bowl. So with that in mind, read the recipe carefully.

	Butter
3	tablespoons flour
1	cup milk, hot
	Salt
	Cayenne pepper
	Worcestershire sauce
1½	cups grated cheddar
4	eggs, separated
1	additional egg white

Preheat oven to 400°. Measure out all ingredients. Butter a 1½-quart soufflé dish. Have a clean dry bowl ready, big enough in which to beat the five egg whites and to contain eventually the whole soufflé mixture with room to spare.

Melt 3 tablespoons butter in the saucepan and stir in flour. Cook over moderate heat, stirring constantly, for 2–3 minutes until the mixture bubbles a bit; do not let it brown.

Remove from heat. When bubbling stops, add hot milk all at once and whisk rapidly until smooth. Beat in ½ teaspoon salt, a dash of cayenne, and 2–3 drops Worcestershire sauce, and add cheese. Stir until cheese is melted.

Add yolks to the cheese mixture one at a time, beating thoroughly after each addition.

Put the egg whites in the bowl. Add a pinch of salt and beat until stiff but not dry. It is perfectly all right to use an electric hand beater. Stir a couple of spoonfuls of the whites into the cheese mixture to lighten it, then add mixture to whites and carefully fold in. Turn into the buttered dish and put in the middle of the oven. Immediately turn the heat down to 350° and cook for 30–35 minutes or until the top is nicely browned and the soufflé puffed. (This extra bit of heat at the very beginning gives the whites an additional boost.)

Serve immediately. Serves 6 as a first course, 4 as a main dish at lunch.

Pita bread with chives

Make pita bread according to the directions given for crisp pita bread (see Index), but mash a stick of room-temperature butter on a plate and blend in 3 tablespoons chopped chives.

Poached peaches...

1½   quarts water
1½   cups sugar
2   tablespoons vanilla extract
6–8 medium-size, firm ripe peaches

Combine water, sugar, and vanilla in a saucepan large enough to hold all the peaches. Make a syrup by simmering a few minutes, stirring until the sugar is dissolved.

Add peaches to syrup and cook at a very gentle simmer, uncovered, for about 10 minutes. Remove peaches with a slotted spoon and drain on a rack. Peel while still warm, then chill. Serve masked with raspberry sauce.

Note: Syrup may be refrigerated and re-used for poaching fruit

... with raspberry sauce

2   10-ounce packages frozen raspberries, thawed
⅔   cup sugar
2   tablespoons Cointreau (optional)

Drain raspberries of syrup. (Reserve syrup for another use, such as a drink or a gelatin dessert). Push them through a sieve and put the puree in a blender jar with sugar. Cover and blend on high speed for 3 minutes or until sugar has dissolved. Add Cointreau if desired. Yield: Approximately 1 cup.

Nut cookies

½   cup butter
1½ cups light brown sugar
1   egg, well beaten
¼   teaspoon salt
1   teaspoon vanilla
3   tablespoons flour
2   cups chopped nuts (pecans or walnuts)

Preheat oven to 325°.

Line baking sheet with aluminum foil.

Cream the butter with the sugar, then add the egg, salt, and flour, and mix well. Fold in the chopped nuts. Drop by teaspoons onto baking sheet. Bake until light brown (8–10 minutes). Cool on baking sheet 5 minutes, then remove with a spatula to a wire rack until completely cooled. Store in tightly covered jars. Makes about 5 dozen cookies.

Note: Do not attempt these cookies on a damp or humid day.

Ohio steamboat hash

SUNDAY BRUNCH OR LATE SUPPER FOR A LAST-MINUTE CROWD

*Ohio steamboat hash

*Broiled tomatoes

Hot rolls

Mixed green salad

*Baked apples with cream

Sour cream coffee cake (see p. 38)

Coffee

Hash made with leftover roast beef or corned beef, topped with a fried egg and served for breakfast, has a long tradition in this country. Unlike the typical hash, this old family recipe is made with fresh meat and can be made in large quantity by tripling the amounts and turning into a casserole after the initial browning of the meat. Baked in a 350° oven for an hour or until the top is browned a bit, it then requires no more attention than being kept warm until all the guests are assembled.

1	pound ground chuck (slightly fatty since no oil or fat of any kind is used in this recipe)
2	medium potatoes, peeled and grated (use unpeeled if the skins are tender)
1	large onion, grated
	Dried oregano
	Salt and freshly ground pepper
1	can beer, at room temperature

Sauté beef in a heavy skillet, without added fat, stirring occasionally until pink has just disappeared. Add potatoes and onion; add oregano, salt, and pepper to taste; stir occasionally. Add beer a little at a time. Cook uncovered over medium heat for about 45 minutes. Serves 4.

Broiled tomatoes

Allow one tomato half per person. Slice tomatoes in two and cut off stem ends so they can stand level. Sprinkle with salt and turn halves upside down on a rack to drain for 15 minutes.

Preheat oven to 350°. Rub halves all over with melted butter, season with pepper and a little brown sugar on the cut side and put on a greased baking sheet. Bake for 15 minutes, then run under broiler briefly to brown. Sprinkle with chopped parsley.

Baked apples with cream

Allowing 1 washed apple per person, take out cores with an apple corer and remove a 1-inch band of skin around top of each. Fill cavities with 1 tablespoon brown sugar and a dash each of cinnamon and nutmeg, and top each with a tablespoon of butter. Put in a baking dish and surround by ½ inch of water. Bake in a preheated 350° oven for about 30 minutes or until apples are tender but not mushy. Baste occasionally.

EAST *Lunches* HAMPTON

Quick cream of tomato soup

This very simple recipe, which tastes quite special, originally came from Greta Garbo.

1	can Campbell's condensed tomato soup
½	can water
1	bay leaf
	Freshly ground pepper
1	scant teaspoon sugar
1	ripe tomato, finely chopped
1	cup heavy cream
½	cup watercress, chopped (leaves and stems)

Put soup and water in an enamel or stainless steel saucepan. Heat briefly, add the bay leaf, pepper, and sugar and stir to blend. Bring to the boil. Add chopped tomato and simmer until tomato is cooked, about 10 minutes. Add cream and heat briefly. Do not boil. Remove bay leaf and serve in heated soup plates. Garnish with watercress. Serves 4–6.

Clam pie

There probably is no dish more characteristic of eastern Long Island than clam pie. The ingredients vary slightly from one cook to another and the clams can be hard [quahogs] or soft. Here are three worthy versions: one with potatoes, one without, and one that was served at the old Sea Spray Inn in East Hampton that is more like a pot pie because it has no bottom crust. Clam pies take very well to freezing and make an ideal light supper or lunch.

Clam pie 1

18–24 medium clams (cherrystones)
12–15 unsalted crackers, crumbled
1 medium onion, finely chopped
4 tablespoons butter, melted
2 teaspoons minute tapioca
½–¾ cup clam liquor
3 slices bacon, cooked, well drained, and crumbled
1 tablespoon chopped parsley
½ teaspoon dried thyme
   Freshly ground black pepper
1 recipe basic pie pastry (see Index)

Preheat oven to 400°.

Chop clams very fine by hand or in a food processor. Combine them well with cracker crumbs, onion, 2 tablespoons butter, tapioca, clam liquor, bacon, parsley, thyme, and pepper to taste. Let mixture stand while you prepare pie pastry. Divide pastry and roll out a 12–13-inch circle for bottom, and a 10-inch circle for top. Line a 9-inch pie pan with the pastry, fill with the clam mixture, dot with remaining butter, and put on the pastry top. Crimp the edges and make a few slits to let steam escape. Bake at 400° for 10 minutes, then lower heat to 350° and bake 35–40 minutes. Serve piping hot. Serves 4–6.

Clam pie II

2	cups clams, coarsely chopped
1	medium onion, coarsely chopped
1	small potato, peeled and cut in large dice
1	egg
¼	cup heavy cream
1	tablespoon melted butter
¾	teaspoon poultry seasoning
	Freshly ground black pepper
1	recipe basic pie pastry (see Index)

Preheat oven to 400°.

Put clams, onion, and potato through the meat grinder. Beat the egg and add to clam mixture with the cream, melted butter, poultry seasoning, and pepper to taste. Divide pastry and roll out a 12–13-inch circle for bottom, and a 10-inch circle for top. Line a 9-inch pie plate with larger circle and pour filling into prepared pie plate, cover with the top crust, and bake for 20–25 minutes, until crust is golden brown. Serves 4–6.

Clam pie III

2   large Long Island potatoes, peeled and sliced
1   large onion, sliced
1   dozen hard clams, minced, with juice reserved
1   small green pepper, seeds and ribs removed, grated
¼   pound bacon, cooked, drained, and finely diced
2   tablespoons chopped parsley
     Salt, freshly ground pepper
     Butter for pie pan
½   recipe basic pie pastry (see Index)

Preheat oven to 400°.

Steam potatoes and onions together in the clam juice until just tender. Add a little water if necessary, but use as little liquid as possible. Drain and set aside.

Mix the clams, green pepper, bacon, parsley, and salt and pepper to taste.

Lightly butter an 8-inch pie dish. Make a layer of the potato-onion mixture, then the clam mixture, and repeat the layers until the dish is full.

Roll out the crust, put on top of filling, and bake until crust is golden brown.

This pie is better when reheated and eaten the day after it is made. Serves 4.

Note: One school of East Hampton clam-pie fanciers likes leftover chicken gravy poured over its pies.

Beach plum pudding

Beach-plumming in early September is an old and pleasant East Hampton custom. After the jelly and jam have been made, any remaining fruit may be frozen for winter desserts. Simply pit the plums with a cherry pitter and pack into plastic freezer jars. No sugar or syrup is needed.

	Butter for pan
1½	cups sugar
2	tablespoons butter
2	eggs, lightly beaten
1	teaspoon vanilla
1½	cups milk
2	cups flour
¼	teaspoon salt
3	teaspoons baking powder
1	cup pitted beach plums

SAUCE:

2	tablespoons butter
2	cups water
2	tablespoons cornstarch
1	cup sugar
½	cup pitted beach plums
1	teaspoon vanilla

Preheat oven to 350°. Butter a 9- × 13-inch Pyrex baking dish.

Cream the butter and sugar together. Add the beaten eggs, vanilla, and milk. Sift together the flour, salt, and baking powder. Combine the two mixtures. Roll beach plums in some additional flour to coat them and stir in. Pour into prepared baking dish and bake for 30 minutes.

While pudding is baking, make sauce:

Melt butter in water in a saucepan. Combine cornstarch and sugar and add. Add beach plums and cook over moderate heat until sauce is thickened. Remove from heat and add vanilla. Serve warm, over warm beach plum pudding. Serves 8–10.

Hot asparagus salad

This dish also makes a nice first course at dinner.

6   slices bacon, diced
1   pound asparagus, preferably medium-size
1   cup wine vinegar
1   tablespoon sugar
¼   teaspoon dry mustard
    Salt and freshly ground pepper
1   quart shredded lettuce leaves (Boston or romaine)
2   hard-cooked eggs, chopped

Fry bacon bits in a skillet until crisp. Remove with a slotted spoon and reserve. Pour off all but 2 tablespoons of the drippings from the pan and discard.

Trim asparagus and cut off tips. Cut stems on the diagonal into pieces 1 inch long. Add stems to skillet and cook over medium high heat stirring constantly until they are crisply tender and bright green—about 5 minutes. Add tips and cook 1 minute longer.

Add vinegar, sugar, mustard, and salt and pepper. Then heat to boiling while stirring. Add bacon bits. Put lettuce in a warmed bowl. Pour asparagus mixture over. Sprinkle with eggs, toss, and serve warm. Serves 3–4 as a main course, 4–6 as a first course.

SPRING LUNCH

*Hot asparagus salad

Warm sourdough bread

*Lady Mendl's bread-and-butter pudding

Lady Mendl's bread & butter pudding

4	half-inch slices good homestyle white bread, or 8 slices good French bread
	Butter at room temperature
	Cinnamon
½	cup golden sultana raisins, soaked for 30 minutes in sherry and drained
¼	cup finely chopped citron, soaked and drained as raisins (optional)
5	eggs
⅔	cup sugar
	Salt
3	cups milk, scalded
1	teaspoon vanilla

Preheat oven to 375°.

Trim crusts off bread; butter one side generously and cut each piece into quarters if using regular bread, into halves if using French bread.

Butter an 8-inch Pyrex baking dish or an oval gratin dish, arrange half the slices in it, and sprinkle sparingly with cinnamon. Strew with drained raisins and citron. Add remaining bread pieces and dust those lightly with cinnamon.

Beat eggs with sugar and a pinch of salt until they are pale yellow. Pour milk in very gradually, working constantly. Stir in vanilla and strain the egg mixture over bread slices. Let stand 15 minutes, then put baking dish in a pan of hot water and bake until the custard is set and a knife inserted in center comes out clean, about 45 minutes. Serve slightly warm with cream. Serves 6–8.

Note: For another, richer version of bread-and-butter pudding you can substitute 1 cup of cream for 1 cup of the milk. Omit the raisins and optional citron and serve with a cold Raspberry Sauce (see p. 14).

Salade niçoise

For best results this salad must be dressed and assembled at the last minute, although all the ingredients can be gathered and partially prepared in advance.

1   cup vinaigrette dressing (see p. 237)
1   pound green beans, blanched for 5 minutes, then rinsed in cold water 2–3 minutes and drained, at room temperature
3   ripe tomatoes, quartered
1   head lettuce, Boston or romaine
2   cups cold French Potato Salad made without onions (see p. 42)
7½ ounces tuna, packed in olive oil, drained
3   hard-cooked eggs, quartered
½   purple onion, cut in paper-thin rings
    2-ounce tin flat anchovy fillets, drained
½   green pepper, cut in thin rings (optional)
4   ounces small black olives, preferably oil-cured

Toss the green beans with several tablespoons of the dressing. Do the same with the tomatoes in a separate bowl.

Just before serving toss the lettuce with about ¼ cup of the dressing, then line a salad bowl with it. Mound the potato salad in the center of the bowl and arrange the beans, tomatoes, tuna, and eggs in clusters or any design you wish around the potato salad. Lay the anchovies over and add the onion rings and green pepper rings if desired. Decorate with the black olives. Spoon the remaining dressing over all and serve. Serves 4–6.

SIMPLE SUMMER LUNCH I

*Salade niçoise

*Cold corn and tomato soup

*Strawberries with crème fraiche

Cold corn and tomato soup

3   cups chicken stock or broth
3   cups cooked corn kernels
1½   cups tomatoes, peeled, seeded, and chopped
1   medium onion, chopped
1   bay leaf
       Salt and white pepper to taste
       Pinch sugar

Combine all the ingredients in a saucepan and bring to a boil, lower heat and simmer, partially covered, for 20 minutes. Cool slightly, then puree in a blender. (You may have to do it in 2 batches.)

Strain, correct seasoning, and chill well. Serves 6–8.

Strawberries with crème fraiche

Pass a bowl of handsome fresh strawberries with separate small bowls of crème fraiche (see Index) and light brown sugar.

SIMPLE SUMMER LUNCH II

*Oeufs mayonnaise

*Tomato salad with basil

French bread, butter

Fresh summer fruits

This deceptively simple meal is extremely satisfying, easy and quick to assemble, and ideal for a hot summer day's lunch served under trees or an umbrella. The eggs can be prepared and the tomatoes done an hour before serving, the basil added at the last minute. A good crusty bread is essential, as both the tomato dressing and the mayonnaise make delectable "mop-ups." A well-chilled light white wine adds a particularly pleasant note.

Oeufs mayonnaise

Oeufs mayonnaise are simply hard-cooked eggs in mayonnaise, preferably a good homemade one (see Index). The eggs can be cooked early in the day or even the night before. Slice them in half lengthwise and arrange them, cut side down, in any pretty serving dish, ideally an oval one. Completely mask them with mayonnaise and dust them with a bit of paprika.

Tomato salad with basil

The combination of fresh tomatoes and fresh basil is one of the great simple joys of summer. The tomatoes must be real ones, not the flannelly pink horrors found in most markets, and ideally for this salad they should be just ripe, but not overripe. Also, only fresh basil will do for this recipe.

A word of warning: When using fresh basil—leaves only! The stems are a purgative!

4–6	vine-ripened tomatoes
	Salt, freshly ground pepper
½	cup good olive oil
1	tablespoon wine vinegar (red or white)
	Handful basil leaves

Cut tomatoes in slices about ⅓ inch thick. Sprinkle with salt and pepper. Dress with olive oil and vinegar about an hour before serving. Refrigerate. Five minutes before serving, chop basil leaves fairly finely and sprinkle on top.

Tortilla española

EARLY SUMMER LUNCH

*Tortilla española

Sliced tomatoes vinaigrette

French bread or rolls

*Sangría

Iced cherries

The tortilla española is a wonderfully versatile dish that can almost be defined by what it is not: It is not a Spanish omelet (which is generally understood to be eggs in combination with green and red peppers) nor does it have anything to do with the Mexican tortilla, which is a flat corn bread. It is, in fact, a thick round cake-like omelet containing only eggs, potatoes, and onions, and is one of the most ubiquitous dishes in Spain. It is common as a first-course dish in Spanish homes, eaten cold; it is a popular picnic dish; and it is also carried by travelers to be eaten in buses and trains. It is carried to the fields by peasants for lunch and sold by the wedge in snack bars. In addition, cut in squares and served with toothpicks, it appears at cocktail parties.

3–4	large potatoes
2–3	medium onions
	Olive oil
	Salt
8–10	eggs
	Freshly ground pepper

Cut potatoes into ½-inch slices, then dice them. Chop the onions coarsely. Heat about ¼ cup olive oil in a heavy skillet (ideally one that is 10 inches in diameter with sloping sides), and sauté the potatoes and onions for 5 minutes over fairly high heat, stirring frequently with a wooden spoon to prevent sticking.

Sprinkle with salt to taste. Cover and continue cooking over low heat, stirring occasionally, for about 10 minutes, or until the potatoes are soft and the onions transparent, but not brown.

Beat the eggs in a large bowl and season with salt and pepper. Remove the potato mixture from the pan with a slotted spoon, stir into the eggs, and let sit 5 minutes or so.

Pour off all but a little of the oil in the pan, heat until

almost smoking, and pour in the egg mixture, shaking the pan all the time so it does not stick. Cook briefly and keep the eggs moving. When the eggs bubble up around the edges of the pan, flatten them quickly with the tip of a fork.

Slide the omelet onto a flat plate, cooked side down. Invert a second plate over the first and, holding the two plates firmly, invert again. The uncooked side is now down. Slide back into the pan and cook as before for another 2 to 3 minutes, to brown the second side.

(The above maneuver is scorned by Spanish chefs, who merely flip the whole thing up and over in the air. We do not recommend this.)

You should now have a round cake ¾-inch to 1-inch thick, firm and slightly brown on the outside, but soft and tender, though not wet, inside. Slide it onto a serving plate. When it has cooled completely, cut into wedges or squares and serve. Serves 6.

(Spanish wine punch)

1	bottle red wine (preferably Burgundy, domestic or French Beaujolais or Spanish Rioja)
1	cup orange juice
½	cup sugar, or to taste
¼	cup Cointreau
1	thinly sliced orange
1	thinly sliced peach (optional)
½	apple, skin on, cubed (optional)
1	pint club soda
	Additional orange slices (optional)

Mix wine, juice, sugar, liqueur, and fruits, and refrigerate for at least an hour before serving to allow fruits to macerate a bit. Add soda and taste for sweetness. Serve in a large pitcher, with ice-filled glasses garnished with an additional slice of orange, if desired.

HOT WEATHER LUNCH OR PICNIC

*Cold sliced filet of beef

Variety of flavored mustards

Cornichons

Salade russe (see p. 35)

Bread, crackers

Assortment of cheeses

*Devil's food cake with
*Chocolate frosting

Cold sliced filet of beef

Have butcher trim a 6-pound filet and tie it every 2 inches or so. Have it at room temperature before going into oven. Preheat oven to 425°.

Rub beef with coarse salt, fresh pepper, and a little dried thyme, if you like. Roast on a rack in preheated oven 6 minutes per pound or until a meat thermometer registers 120°. Cool and serve at room temperature. If at all possible, avoid refrigerating.

Devil's food cake

2   cups sugar
1   cup milk
4   1-ounce squares unsweetened chocolate
2   eggs, lightly beaten, and 2 eggs, separated
1½   sticks butter, at room temperature
2   cups cake flour
¾   teaspoon soda
½   teaspoon baking powder
1   tablespoon vanilla
       Chocolate frosting (see next recipe)

Preheat oven to 350°.

Butter and flour two square 8-inch pans and line with buttered waxed paper.

Put 1 cup of the sugar, the milk, chocolate, and 2 of the eggs in the top of a double boiler. Cook, stirring constantly, over simmering water until mixture has thickened.

32   LUNCHES

Remove from heat and let cool. Cream butter, add 1 cup sugar, then the 2 egg yolks, one at a time.

Sift together flour, soda, and baking powder. Add flour mixture and chocolate mixture alternately to the butter-sugar mixture, a little of each at a time, blending well after each addition. Stir in vanilla.

Beat the 2 egg whites until stiff but not dry, and fold into batter. Pour batter into the prepared pans and bake for 25 minutes or until a tester comes out clean. Set pans on wire racks for 5 minutes to cool, then turn cakes out on racks and cool completely. Frost with chocolate frosting. Serves 8–10.

Chocolate frosting

4	squares unsweetened chocolate
1	cup sifted confectioner's sugar
2	tablespoons hot water
2	egg yolks
½	teaspoon vanilla extract
1	tablespoon soft butter
¼	cup milk

Melt chocolate in a double boiler or by placing in a small Pyrex dish in the oven. Beat in sugar and hot water; blend well. Add egg yolks, one at a time, beating well after each. Beat in vanilla and milk and continue beating for several minutes until stiff enough to spread. (An electric beater makes the job easier.) Frosting may be refrigerated for a while before spreading.

New potato salad

2   pounds small red-skinned new potatoes, uniformly sized, scrubbed and unpeeled
1/3   cup mayonnaise
1/2   cup low-fat yogurt
2   tablespoons lemon juice
1   tablespoon prepared mustard
2   tablespoons minced shallots or chopped chives
2   tablespoons minced parsley
     Fresh black pepper
     Salt

Boil or steam the potatoes until tender. When cool enough to handle yet still warm, cut into halves and place in a bowl. Do not skin. Mix together the remaining ingredients, pour over the potatoes, and toss well. Season to taste with several grindings of black pepper and salt if desired. Refrigerate 1 to 2 hours before serving. Serves 6.

Cold salmon mousse

1   packet unflavored gelatin
3   tablespoons lemon juice
1/2   small onion, cut up
1/2   cup boiling water
1/2   cup mayonnaise
2   cups cooked fresh salmon or one 1-pound can, drained
1/4   teaspoon paprika
1   cup heavy cream
1   tablespoon chopped fresh dill
     Watercress
     Thin lemon slices
     Salade russe (see p. 35)

Put gelatin, lemon juice, onion, and boiling water in blender or food processor container; cover and blend at high speed for 40 seconds. Add mayonnaise, salmon, paprika, and dill; blend briefly. Add cream gradually while blending 30 seconds more. Pour into a 4-cup 12-inch-diameter ring mold and chill until mousse is firm and set.

Unmold onto a serving platter. Garnish with watercress and thin lemon slices. If desired, fill center with salade russe. Serves 6–8.

Salade russe

	Salt
2	10-ounce boxes frozen peas, partly defrosted
2	10-ounce boxes frozen baby lima beans, partly defrosted
4–6	carrots, cut in medium dice
¼	cup finely minced onion
2	tablespoons lemon juice
⅔	cup mayonnaise
¼	teaspoon white pepper
2	teaspoons sugar
	Handful finely chopped dill

Bring 2 cups of salted water to a boil in a large pot; add the peas and limas a box at a time, allowing the water to return to the boil each time. Cover, lower fire, and cook 7 minutes. Drain in a colander and run cold water over. Allow vegetables to cool while you make the sauce.

Beat the lemon juice into the mayonnaise with 1 teaspoon salt, the pepper, and sugar.

Put cooled peas and lima beans in a large mixing bowl. Add diced carrots and onion. Pour sauce over vegetables and stir in gently. Add dill and mix again. Cover tightly with plastic wrap and refrigerate for several hours before serving.

This recipe can be halved. Serves 10–12.

Beach plum pie

(*LVIS Cookbook*, 1939)

Prepare one recipe basic pie pastry for top and bottom crusts (see Index). Slip pits from enough fresh beach plums to fill the pie plate, add sugar and flour in the following proportions: To 1 cup pitted plums packed solid, ¾ cup sugar mixed with 1 teaspoon flour. Mix well, bake in a preheated 350° oven until brown. Canned beach plums may be used. Drain off juice, adding 2 teaspoons flour to 3 cups drained beach plums; then put back juice needed.

Chicken salad

1	large stewing chicken (fowl), cut up
2–3	ribs celery
1	carrot
2	leeks or 1 large onion
1	bay leaf
6–8	peppercorns
	Several parsley stems
	Salt
1	cup celery, chopped
¼	cup shallots or scallions, minced
	Mayonnaise (preferably homemade)
	Hard-cooked eggs, quartered
	Cherry tomatoes
	Olives
	Watercress

Cook the thighs and legs of the chicken first; put them in a large kettle with the celery, carrot, leeks or onion, bay leaf, peppercorns, and parsley stems with cold water to

---

PICNIC UNDER THE TREES

*Chicken salad

*Coleslaw

Thin roast beef sandwiches with *Horseradish mayonnaise (see p. 236)

Pickles

Cherry tomatoes

Hard-cooked eggs with salt, pepper, and chopped chives for dipping

*Sour cream coffee cake

Watermelon slices

cover. Simmer for 30 minutes, then add the rest of the chicken and continue cooking until the white meat is tender, approximately another 40 minutes. The liquid should simmer, not boil, or the broth, which you can save for other purposes, will be cloudy.

Cool chicken in broth, then remove. Strain broth and reserve. Tear chicken to bite-size pieces, add the chopped celery and shallots or scallions, toss with enough mayonnaise to bind, and chill. Garnish with egg quarters, cherry tomatoes, olives, watercress—any or all. Serves 8.

Note: Add ½ cup chopped walnuts for an interesting taste and texture variation.

Coleslaw

1	medium head firm green cabbage
1	small onion
2	carrots, peeled
½	green pepper

DRESSING:

6	tablespoons mayonnaise
3	tablespoons cider vinegar
1	tablespoon salt
2	teaspoons sugar
2	teaspoons celery seeds
	Heavy cream (optional)

Cut cabbage in quarters. Remove hearts. Shred on a slaw grater, or with a knife or the slicing disc of a food processor. Grate onion, carrots, and green pepper over cabbage and mix thoroughly with hands. Combine dressing ingredients, thin with a little cream or milk if desired, pour over shredded vegetables, mix thoroughly, and refrigerate for several hours before serving. Serves 8.

Sour cream coffee cake

½   pound butter, softened
1¾   cups sugar
3   eggs
3   cups flour
      Salt
1   tablespoon baking powder
1   teaspoon baking soda
1   cup sour cream
1   teaspoon vanilla
1   teaspoon cinnamon
½   cup chopped walnuts
      Butter for pan

Preheat oven to 350°. Cream the butter with 1 cup of the sugar until light and fluffy. Beat in the eggs one at a time. Sift the flour, ½ teaspoon salt, baking powder, and baking soda and add, blending well. Mix in the sour cream and the vanilla.

In a small bowl blend the remaining ¾ cup sugar with a pinch of salt, cinnamon, and the walnuts. Set aside.

Butter a 10-inch tubular springform pan with removable sides. Pour ⅓ of the batter into the pan and smooth it out with a spatula. Sprinkle ⅓ of the cinnamon mixture over the batter. Repeat these layers twice, smoothing out the batter each time. Bake at 350° for 50 minutes. Cool for ½ hour in the tin, then remove side and place on a rack to cool completely before removing bottom and cutting.

Note: This cake freezes very well.

Deviled eggs

8   eggs, hard-cooked and peeled
½   medium onion, minced
2   tablespoons pickle relish
½   teaspoon Dijon mustard
        Salt
        Cayenne
        Mayonnaise
        Paprika
        Small parsley sprigs (optional)

Halve eggs lengthwise. Scoop out the yolks, mash lightly with a fork, and add the onion, pickle, relish, mustard, salt to taste, and a dash of cayenne. Mix with just enough mayonnaise to bind, and pile back into the white halves. Sprinkle lightly with paprika and decorate with a small parsley sprig if desired. Serves 8–10.

Perfect roast chicken

Put 1 teaspoon dried tarragon (or several branches fresh) inside a washed and dried 3½-pound roasting chicken. Salt and pepper the inside and add a good lump of butter. Truss well, smear softened butter or olive oil on the outside and salt and pepper the skin. Roast bird breast *down* at 475° for 45 minutes. Cut into serving pieces with a poultry shears. Serves 4. Roast 2 birds for 8.

Note: It may be a bit smoky, but this method yields a beautifully golden moist bird.
    For a picnic, cook chicken in the morning and serve at room temperature (try not to refrigerate it).

PICNIC AT THE BEACH

*Deviled eggs

*Perfect roast chicken

Purple onion and mayonnaise sandwiches

*White bean salad

Ripe tomato quarters

Peaches, plums, and nectarines

*Pecan tartlets

Iced tea and iced coffee

White bean salad

2   cups (1 pound) dried small white pea beans
1   medium onion
4–5   cloves
½   cup olive oil
¼   cup lemon juice
2   cloves garlic, minced
4   scallions, white and part of the green, finely chopped
¼   cup chopped parsley
¼   cup minced dill, or more
        Salt and freshly ground pepper

Soak beans in water overnight, or boil 2 minutes and then soak 1 hour. Discard soaking water. Stud onion with cloves and add to beans along with water to cover. Bring to a boil, cover, and simmer 1½–2 hours, or until tender. Drain well and cool to lukewarm. Beat oil and lemon juice together and toss with beans, along with garlic, scallions, parsley, dill, and salt and pepper to taste. Refrigerate for at least 3 hours and sprinkle with additional dill, if desired, before serving. Serves 8–10.

Pecan tartlets

To make individual pecan tartlets for a picnic or large party, use the pecan pie recipe (see Index) but make them in shallow muffin tins. Line each cup of the tin with pastry as you would the pie plate. Fill with pecan mixture and bake in a preheated 350° oven for 25–30 minutes. Lower the heat to 250° and bake 10 minutes more. Cool before removing from tin.

One regular pie recipe will make 16 dessert tartlets. These can be made in quantity 2 to 3 days in advance.

Cold poached salmon

3-pound piece of fresh salmon fillet (approximate weight)

Court bouillon:
2   pounds fresh fish bones, heads, etc.
1   bay leaf
1   onion stuck with 2 cloves
2   ribs celery
2   tablespoons salt
8–10 peppercorns
2   cups dry white wine

Make a court bouillon (poaching broth) by combining the fish bones, etc., bay leaf, onion, celery, salt, and pepper in a large pot. Add enough water so that fish bones are covered. Bring to a boil, cover, and cook 20 minutes. Correct seasoning, add wine, and cook uncovered for 5 minutes more. Strain.

To poach fish: Wrap salmon in a length of cheesecloth and put in boiling court bouillon. Cover, lower heat, and cook 8 minutes per pound if the fillet is thick; 5–6 if it is thin. Adjust heat so liquid just shudders—slightly less than a simmer.

Let the fish cool in the liquid, then remove, unwrap carefully and, as salmon is most flavorful at room temperature, keep cool but not refrigerated if possible. Serves 8–10.

BUFFET LUNCH

*Cold poached salmon

*Sauce verte

*French potato salad

*Cucumber salad (see p. 145)

French bread

*Lemon mousse

Sauce verte

(green mayonnaise)

2	cups mayonnaise (see Index)
½	bunch watercress
½	bunch parsley
1	tablespoon chopped fresh tarragon
1	tablespoon chopped fresh chives or scallion tops
1	teaspoon chopped fresh dill
	Salt, freshly ground pepper

Remove stems from watercress and parsley. Chop very fine and twist in cheesecloth or the corner of a dish towel to remove excess liquid. Combine with the tarragon and chives or scallion tops, and mix well into mayonnaise. Season to taste.

Note: ½ cup of finely chopped spinach may be used instead of the watercress, for a deeper green mayonnaise.

French potato salad

(potatoes in oil and vinegar)

5–6	medium potatoes, skins on, scrubbed
	Salt
¼	cup chicken broth or stock
⅓	cup vinaigrette dressing (see Index)
2	tablespoons minced shallots or purple onion
3	tablespoons chopped parsley

Place potatoes in boiling salted water to cover and cook until just tender. Do not overcook or salad will be mushy.

Drain potatoes and when they can be handled, peel them. Cut into ¼-inch slices and immediately pour chicken broth over the still warm slices; toss gently. Let sit a few minutes so potatoes can absorb broth.

Pour vinaigrette dressing over and add shallots or onion and parsley. Toss again gently and serve. Serves 4–6.

Lemon mousse

The unusually intense lemon flavor of this mousse, plus its lightness, make it possibly the best lemon mousse ever. It uses a large amount of lemon zest (colored skin) and juice, plus very little gelatin. Special care must be taken to make sure the soaked gelatin is completely dissolved throughout the hot mixture. (see Index: to clarify gelatin)

1	packet unflavored gelatin
5	tablespoons grated lemon rind
1	cup lemon juice
8	eggs (preferably at room temperature—they separate easier)
2	cups sugar
½	teaspoon salt
2	cups heavy cream

Dissolve gelatin according to directions. Grate lemon zest, then squeeze lemons to extract juice.

Separate eggs, dropping the whites into a good-size mixing bowl, and the yolks directly into the top of a large double boiler. Add lemon juice, 1 cup of the sugar, and salt to yolks. Cook over boiling water, stirring constantly, until slightly thick and custardy. Stir in zest and then gelatin, making sure to blend thoroughly. Let cool about 10 minutes.

Pour cooled lemon mixture into a very large mixing bowl in which all ingredients can be combined. Beat cream until it holds its shape. Fold it into lemon mixture. Beat egg whites until they form soft peaks, then gradually add remaining cup of sugar and continue beating until mixture forms stiff peaks. Fold whites with a wire whisk, a little at a time, into lemon and cream mixture, using a strong wrist motion to make sure to blend in lemon mixture from the bottom. Don't rush the final folding. It must be thorough. Pour into a large glass serving bowl or soufflé dish and chill, covered with plastic wrap, overnight. Serves 8–10.

Note: This recipe can easily be halved.

Nora Bennett's clam chowder

This clam chowder is not for everyone, being a two-day affair; but if you have the time, the result is incredibly good.

1½	quarts fresh chowder clams (measured without liquid)
3	cups fresh clam juice reserved from the clams
3	cups water
4–5	stalks celery
3–4	carrots
4–5	medium onions
6	medium potatoes, peeled
1	can tomatoes (16 ounces)
6	tablespoons butter
1½	cups milk with 3 tablespoons removed
3	tablespoons heavy cream
	Salt, freshly ground pepper

Rinse clams, chop coarsely by hand or with several pulses of a food processor.

Put clam juice and water in a large kettle and bring to the simmer.

Grind celery, carrots, onions and potatoes. Mix and add to the kettle. Add half of the clams and refrigerate the other half. Add the tomatoes, butter, and salt and pepper

FALL LUNCH
━━━━━

*Clam chowder

Warmed pilot crackers

Mixed green salad

*Apple pie

to taste. Bring to a boil, partially cover, lower heat, and simmer for 7 hours, adding the milk after 3 hours.

Watch that chowder does not boil (an asbestos pad may be necessary) and stir occasionally (if at any time the chowder appears too thick, you can thin it with a little water).

Cool and refrigerate overnight. Before serving time add the reserved clams and the heavy cream. Heat for about 15 minutes but do not boil. Correct seasonings and serve in heated soup plates. Serves 8.

Note: This chowder freezes well.

Clam chowder

4	large potatoes
½	pound very lean bacon, cut in ¼-inch dice
1	medium onion, minced
2	cups canned cream-style corn
1	can whole corn
2	quarts fish stock, potato water, or chicken broth
1	quart chowder clams plus juice
	Salt and freshly ground pepper
½	cup sliced red pimiento
1	cup cream or milk, heated
	Walnut-size lump of butter (optional)
	Chopped parsley

Peel potatoes, cut in ¾-inch cubes, cover with water, bring to the boil and boil 5 minutes. Drain and set aside.

Cook bacon in big heavy pot, remove with a slotted spoon when crisp, and drain. Keep warm. Cook onions gently in hot fat. When limp, add drained potatoes and mix well. Add corn, mix thoroughly, then add hot stock. Simmer 15 minutes or until potatoes become mushy. Add clams and season to taste with salt and pepper. Heat just enough to blend—do not allow to boil or cook too long, as clams will toughen.

Add pimientos and cream or milk and continue heating. Pour into hot tureen and top with lump of butter if desired. Garnish with bacon and chopped parsley. Serves 4 as a hearty main dish or 8 as a first course.

Apple pie

1	recipe basic pie pastry (see Index)
2	tablespoons flour
1¼	cups sugar
10	medium apples, such as McIntosh, Cortland, or Granny Smith
½	teaspoon cinnamon
¼	teaspoon nutmeg
¼	teaspoon salt
1	cup heavy cream

TOPPING:
1	teaspoon cinnamon and 1 teaspoon sugar, mixed.

Preheat oven to 450°.

Roll out half the pastry and line a 9-inch pie plate with it. Mix 1 tablespoon flour and ¼ cup sugar and sprinkle evenly over bottom. Peel and core apples and, cutting thinly, slice them directly into the prepared pastry shell.

Mix together the remaining sugar and flour, the cinnamon, nutmeg, and salt. Sprinkle over the apples. Slowly pour cream over all. Roll out remaining pastry for top crust, fit into place; trim, moisten edges, and crimp to seal. Cut several slits in top to allow steam to escape, and sprinkle with cinnamon-sugar topping.

Bake at 450° for 15 minutes, then reduce oven heat to 350° and bake 30 minutes more. Let cool for an hour before serving. Serves 6.

Curry of lamb or chicken

A *"westernized"* curry, in which some of the ingredients normally used as curry garnishes, such as apples, bananas, and raisins, are included in the cooking, with very tasty results.

2   tablespoons butter
2   tablespoons oil
2   cups or more leftover lamb or chicken, cubed
1   cup chopped onion
¾   cup chopped celery
1   cup chopped apple
2   firm, ripe bananas, cubed
2   cloves garlic, minced
¼   cup curry powder or to taste
2   tablespoons flour
1   cup diced peeled tomatoes
¼   cup raisins (optional)
1   cup chicken broth or stock
     Salt and pepper
½   cup heavy cream

Heat butter and oil in a large skillet; warm the meat or chicken in it, but do not let meat get hard and brown, then add the onions, apples, celery, bananas, and garlic and cook, stirring, until most of the moisture evaporates.

Sprinkle with the flour and curry and mix well until meat is coated. Add tomatoes, raisins, chicken broth, and salt and pepper and bring to a boil. Stir in the heavy cream and correct seasoning. Serve with rice and, if you like, with additional garnishes such as chutney, mango pickle, or chopped peanuts, although the dish really stands by itself.

Can be made early and kept warm until mealtime. Serves 4.

LUNCH OF LEFTOVERS

*Curry of lamb or chicken

Hot rice

Chutney

*Cucumber raita in *Yogurt

Orange slices with grated coconut, slivered almonds, and Grand Marnier

Cucumber raita

(cucumbers in yogurt)

16   ounces yogurt (commercial or homemade—see below)
1   cucumber
1   teaspoon salt
1   teaspoon ground cumin
     Cayenne pepper
     Chopped parsley

Whip yogurt lightly. Peel and chop the cucumber very fine. Add to the yogurt with the salt and cumin. Sprinkle with cayenne pepper and serve. Makes about 2½ cups.

Yogurt

1   quart regular milk
3   tablespoons plain yogurt

Bring the milk to the boil, then allow to cool to about 130°–150°. (Check temperature with a meat or candy thermometer.)

Put the 3 tablespoons yogurt in a large Pyrex bowl. Add ½ cup of the milk, a spoonful at a time, beating constantly. Then add the rest in a thin stream, still beating constantly.

Cover bowl tightly with plastic wrap, wrap bowl in a bath towel, and leave 8–10 hours in a warm place having a temperature of 85°–95° (an unlit oven heated only by the pilot light is a good place). Pour off the whey, or yellow liquid on top, then refrigerate.

Save 3 tablespoons to make the next batch!

Stracciatelle

(chicken egg drop soup)

3   eggs
2½   tablespoons semolina
4   ounces grated Parmesan cheese
      Dash nutmeg
      Salt and freshly ground pepper
2   quarts chicken broth or stock

Beat eggs until smooth and add semolina, cheese, nutmeg, salt, and pepper. Mix into 2 cups of the stock.

Bring the remaining stock to the boil; while it is boiling, add egg mixture and quickly whisk it in with a wire whisk. Lower heat and simmer gently 2–3 minutes until the eggs break up into little strands (stracciatelle). Serves 4–6.

FALL LUNCH OR LATE SUPPER I

*Stracciatelle

*Risotto with mussels

Endive salad with chopped chives

*Sherry jelly

Risotto with mussels

3 pounds cleaned mussels
¾ cup finely chopped onion
3 tablespoons olive oil
3 tablespoons butter
2 cloves garlic
¼ cup chopped parsley
½ cup dry white wine
  Freshly ground pepper
1¾–2 cups chicken broth
1½ cups Arborio rice
  Freshly grated Parmesan cheese

Open mussels by steaming in a large pot with a lid, over high heat with no water, just a wet tea towel on top. Discard shells and strain liquid through cheesecloth. Reserve liquid.

Sauté onion in oil and butter until lightly golden; add garlic, parsley, wine, and pepper to taste; simmer 5 minutes.

Combine mussel broth and chicken broth in small saucepan, bring to a boil, and keep hot while risotto cooks.

Add about ¾ cup of the broth to the mixture and bring to a boil. Lower flame, add rice, and cook, stirring frequently until all liquid is absorbed (watch so that all the liquid doesn't cook away at any one time or it will burn). Continue adding liquid by small ladlefuls until rice reaches desired degree of doneness (which to Italians is al dente and quite moist). Salt to taste.

Shortly before rice completes cooking, add mussels and stir in. Serve with freshly grated cheese passed separately. Serves 4–6.

Note: The Italian Arborio rice requires a longer cooking time and more cooking liquid than Carolina rice. It can be found in some Italian markets and in most health food stores, and is well worth seeking out. It is "real rice," tasty, chewy, and a delightful surprise after using the tasteless instant kind.

Sherry Jelly

⅔   cup sugar, approximately (see note)
2¼ tablespoons gelatin, soaked in ½ cup cold water
1   cup boiling water
1⅔ cup sherry
⅓   cup freshly squeezed orange juice
3   tablespoons freshly squeezed lemon juice
1   cup heavy cream
      Sugar
½   teaspoon almond extract

Combine sugar and boiling water and pour over well-dissolved gelatin mixture. Stir in sherry and orange and lemon juice. Strain into a mold, bowl, or individual dishes. Chill until set.

Serve with whipped cream sweetened to taste with sugar and flavored with almond extract.

Note: The dryness of the sherry determines the exact amount of sugar needed. A medium sherry is best.

Crab stew

LUNCH OR LATE
SUPPER II

*Crab stew

French bread

Salad of endive and
watercress

*Apricot mousse

This dish has a number of virtues other than being delicious. It can be made to advantage the day before or in the morning and gently reheated. It also travels well. It is delightful at lunch and also makes a light yet satisfying meal before the theater, as well as after.

4	cups chicken broth
½	teaspoon saffron threads or ¼ teaspoon powdered saffron
¼	pound butter, more if necessary
1	cup celery in medium dice
1	cup carrots in medium dice
2	leeks, diced
4	shallots, minced
1	green pepper, seeded and diced
3	tomatoes, peeled, seeded, and diced
¾–1	pound fresh lump crabmeat
2	tablespoons Worcestershire sauce
2	cups cooked rice
	Fresh chopped parsley
	Salt, freshly ground pepper

Heat chicken broth with saffron, skimming fat if necessary.

Melt butter and steam the celery, carrots, leeks, and shallots for 10 minutes. Add the green pepper and continue cooking 5 minutes longer without letting vegetables brown, stirring occasionally.

Add tomatoes and continue steaming, adding butter if necessary.

Pick over crabmeat, removing bits of shell or cartilage. Add to the vegetables with Worcestershire sauce. Cook 5 minutes, stirring. Add saffron broth with salt and pepper. Simmer a few minutes or reheat at serving time.

Place rice (which should be a little undercooked) in a heated dish. Pour hot stew into a heated tureen and sprinkle with parsley. Spoon soup over rice in heated soup plates. Serves 6.

Apricot mousse

1   lemon
1   pound dried apricots (see note) soaked in water for 30 minutes
1   cup applesauce
½   cup sugar or to taste
4   egg whites
      Toasted slivered almonds

Remove zest (colored skin) from lemon in thin strips, using a vegetable peeler. Then extract juice.

Drain apricots and combine in a saucepan with applesauce, julienned zest, and lemon juice. Simmer for 30 minutes, uncovered.

Puree mixture in a blender, put mixture in a bowl, let cool, add sugar to taste.

Beat egg whites until stiff; then put beater in the apricot puree. Whip puree and gradually add egg whites and whip in. Pile mousse in a serving dish and chill. Garnish with almonds. Serves 8.

Note: Unsulfured apricots, available in health food stores, have a much better flavor than the commercial variety. They are worth the extra price.

OTHER MAIN COURSES FOR LUNCH (OR LIGHT SUPPER)

*Bluefish pie

*Quiche Lorraine

*Manicotti

*Baked crab and shrimp

*Salade Dumas

*Croque-monsieur

Bluefish pie

3	slices bacon, cooked and fairly crisp
1	medium onion
16	unsalted crackers
1	fillet of bluefish, skinned (1 to 1½ pounds)
1½	cups milk
1	scant teaspoon minute tapioca
2	tablespoons melted butter
1	tablespoon chopped parsley
½	teaspoon dried thyme
	Salt, freshly ground pepper
1	recipe basic pie pastry (see Index)

Preheat oven to 450°. Bake the pastry shell for 5 minutes.

Put the bacon, onion, crackers, and bluefish in bowl of food processor; process just until finely chopped. Add the milk, tapioca, butter, parsley, thyme, and salt and pepper to taste. Blend mixture and run some through grinder again to clean it out.

Divide pastry in half. Roll out and line a 10-inch pie plate with one half. Add filling. Dot with butter. Fit top crust in place, seal edges, and make several slashes for steam to escape. Bake in the upper third of oven at 450° for 10 minutes, then lower the heat to 350°, and bake for 35–40 minutes, until crust is golden. Serves 6–8.

Quiche Lorraine

1	9-inch unbaked pâté brisée shell (see Index)
6	slices bacon
1	medium onion, chopped
1	teaspoon flour
1	cup grated Gruyère or Swiss cheese
¼	cup grated Parmesan cheese
5	eggs, beaten
1	cup milk
1	cup light cream
¼	teaspoon nutmeg
½	teaspoon salt
½	teaspoon freshly ground white pepper

Preheat oven to 450°.

Bake the pastry shell for 5 minutes.

Cook bacon until crisp. When cool, crumble and set aside.

Sauté onion in 1–2 tablespoons bacon fat until soft and transparent.

Sprinkle bottom of pie shell with flour, then cover with crumbled bacon and onions. Sprinkle grated cheeses over all.

Beat eggs, milk, cream, nutmeg, salt, and pepper together. Strain the mixture over the cheeses. Bake for 15 minutes at 450°; lower temperature down to 350°, and bake 10 minutes longer, or until a knife inserted in center comes out clean. Serves 6–8.

Manicotti

This dish freezes very well and, with the addition of a salad, makes a satisfying meal any time of the year. It is a good thing to have on hand for Sunday night supper, frozen in exactly the quantity you need for a family meal. Of course, large quantities may be made ahead and frozen for a party.

	Olive oil
1	pound mixed chopped veal and pork
16	ounces ricotta cheese
8	ounces mozzarella, chopped into ¼-inch pieces
2	eggs, lightly beaten
¼	cup chopped parsley
¼	teaspoon freshly ground nutmeg
	Salt, freshly ground pepper
18	manicotti shells
4	cups well-seasoned, preferably homemade, tomato sauce (see Index)

½–⅔ cup grated Parmesan cheese

Put on to boil a very large pot of water, in which you will cook the shells, and add several drops of olive oil.

Brown the meat in a skillet and drain well. Set aside.

Mix together the ricotta, mozzarella, eggs, parsley, and nutmeg. Season to taste with salt and pepper, then blend in the meat.

When the water comes to a full rolling boil, add the manicotti shells 3 or 4 at a time. Boil 6 minutes. Run cold water into pot to stop cooking, then remove shells with tongs, and drain.

Select a pan or pans to hold the shells (if you are going to freeze them, 8-inch square aluminum foil pans work well). Pour enough of the tomato sauce in to cover bottom of pan. Stuff each shell with meat mixture, taking care not to break them (a long-handled spoon such as an iced tea spoon is good), and pack tightly into pan in a single layer. Cover well with sauce and sprinkle with grated Parmesan. Wrap well and freeze.

To bake: allow to come to room temperature. Bake in a preheated 350° oven for 40 minutes tightly covered. Then bake an additional 15 minutes, uncovered. (Of course, you may bake them directly, without freezing.) Serves 6–8.

Baked crab and shrimp

1	medium green pepper, finely chopped
1	medium onion, finely chopped
1	cup celery, finely chopped
½	pound crabmeat
½	pound shrimp, coarsely chopped
½	teaspoon Worcestershire sauce
1	cup mayonnaise, preferably homemade (see Index)
1	cup fresh breadcrumbs
4	tablespoons melted butter

Combine green pepper, onion, celery, crabmeat, shrimp, Worcestershire, and mayonnaise in a casserole. Mix breadcrumbs and butter and sprinkle over top of casserole. Bake in a preheated 350° oven for 30 minutes, or until crumbs are browned slightly. Can be prepared ahead. Serves 4.

Salade Dumas

The original version of this salad, also known as Salade Francillon, is said to have originated with Dumas Fils and called for several whole truffles to be gently simmered in champagne and then slivered into the salad. We find it quite good on its own, with just black olives for color, but you can add the truffles if you are feeling flush or unusually Francophilic.

4–5	medium potatoes, unpeeled
2	cups chicken broth
1	quart mussels, steamed (see Note)
½	teaspoon salt
	Several grindings freshly ground black pepper
½	teaspoon dried tarragon (or 1 tablespoon fresh)
2	tablespoons wine vinegar
½	cup dry white wine
6	tablespoons olive oil
4–6	large black olives, slivered

Scrub potatoes and simmer in the chicken broth until tender, about 20 minutes. Peel and slice into a bowl. Add the mussels.

Combine remaining ingredients and pour over potato mixture; toss gently. Chill for 2 to 3 hours. Serves 4–6.

Note: An easy way to steam mussels open after scrubbing and debearding them is to place them in a large covered pot over very high heat with just a kitchen towel wrung out in hot water over them. Shake the pot occasionally and they should open in 8 to 10 minutes. Discard any shells that have remained closed. Remove the mussels from the shells with a sharp knife.

Croque-monsieur

[A pan-grilled ham and cheese sandwich]

Cut off crusts from 2 slices of good sandwich bread. Make a sandwich of 2 slices of boiled ham and a slice of Gruyère or Swiss cheese. Or, if unavailable, use Norwegian Jarlsberg or, as a last resort, American cheese.

Melt 2 tablespoons butter in a heavy skillet and sauté the sandwich on both sides until outsides are crisp and golden brown, the cheese slightly melted. Add more butter if necessary and press sandwich down from time to time with a spatula.

EAST

Dinners

HAMPTON

*I*n the city, prepare the Poulet Gran'mère. Take washed and dried salad greens in a plastic bag. Carry a jar of vinaigrette sauce (see Index) or make it at the last minute. Take a crusty French bread, because the sauce of the chicken begs for dunking, and a good wedge of cheese. Providentially, your country freezer will be stocked with frozen peas to prepare on arrival. Carry fresh ripe pears.

Poulet Gran'mère

6	tablespoons butter
2	tablespoons chopped onion
¼	pound sausage meat
1	chicken liver, chopped
¼	cup fresh bread crumbs
1	4-pound chicken, cleaned
¼	pound salt pork or raw bacon, finely diced
10	small white onions
½	pound potatoes, quartered and parboiled 10 minutes
¼	teaspoon each parsley, rosemary, and thyme
	Salt, freshly ground pepper

Stuffing: Melt 2 tablespoons butter in a large skillet and sauté chopped onion until wilted. Stir in sausage meat, chopped liver, bread crumbs, herbs, and salt and pepper to taste. Cook for 2 minutes, stirring constantly.

Blanch salt pork or bacon, drain and dry on paper towels.

Clean bird, stuff with sausage mixture, and truss. Put in a large heavy casserole with diced salt pork or bacon, onions, and remaining butter. Cover and cook over low heat for 30 minutes. Add quartered potatoes, baste, and cook covered 20 minutes longer, or until potatoes are tender. Serves 4.

EASY FRIDAY
NIGHT DINNER
IN THE COUNTRY

*Poulet Gran'mère

*French peas

Salad of mixed
greens

Crusty French bread

Port Salut cheese
with fresh pears

French peas

(with frozen peas)

Frozen peas can be made to taste more like fresh if you cook them this way: Allow the block to partially defrost so you can break it up. Put peas in a saucepan with ½ cup chicken broth, ½ teaspoon sugar, a good knob of butter, and a pinch of dried thyme. Bring to a boil and simmer covered until peas are tender but not mushy and liquid is almost gone—about 7 minutes. You may wish to cook them over high heat, uncovered, for 2 or 3 additional minutes to evaporate the liquid. Serves 4.

*T*his is another menu that can be prepared ahead with the exception of the pasta, which is cooked at the last minute. The prosciutto should be sliced paper-thin and served with a peppermill; the melon should be cut in wedges.

Chicken in white wine sauce

2	chickens (3 pounds each), cut into 16 pieces each
4–6	tablespoons butter
¼	cup olive oil
	Salt, freshly ground pepper
2–3	onions, chopped
12	fresh mushrooms, sliced
1	teaspoon oregano
3–4	cloves garlic, minced
½–1	cup dry white wine
1	cup chicken broth
1	pound linguini, cooked al dente
	Butter (optional)
½	cup chopped fresh parsley

Dry chicken pieces with paper towels.

Heat 2 tablespoons butter with 2 tablespoons oil and begin browning chicken pieces well, a few at a time. Season them with salt and pepper as they brown. Add more butter and oil as needed, and keep chicken pieces warm as they are set aside, until all are browned.

Add any remaining butter and oil to the pan and sauté onions lightly. Remove onions and set aside.

Add mushrooms, oregano, garlic, and wine to the pan and cook a few minutes.

Add chicken broth, stir and add the chicken pieces and onions. Bring to a simmer, cover, and simmer gently 20–30 minutes.

Remove chicken pieces to a warm platter. Stir sauce, taste for seasoning, and cook for a few minutes, uncovered, to reduce. Swirl in some additional butter if desired.

Put cooked, drained linguini in center of a large warmed deep platter.

Pour sauce over. Surround with chicken pieces and sprinkle with parsley. Serves 6.

Mustard-baked chicken

3½	pound frying chicken, cut into 8 pieces
¼	pound unsalted butter
	Juice of 1 medium lemon
	Butter for baking dish
	Salt, freshly ground pepper
	Dijon-type mustard
1	egg, beaten with 1 tablespoon water
¾	cup bread crumbs
¼	teaspoon dried tarragon
	Paprika

Preheat oven to 350°.
Melt butter with the lemon juice and set aside to cool. Butter a baking dish or dishes large enough to hold all the chicken pieces in one layer.

Season chicken pieces well on both sides with salt and pepper. Brush parts thickly with mustard on both sides (use a basting brush or an inexpensive small paintbrush). Dip each piece in egg and allow excess to drip off.

Mix bread crumbs, salt and pepper to taste, and tarragon on a plate. Roll chicken piece in mixture to coat and arrange in buttered baking dish. Spread cooled and slightly thickened butter mixture over chicken, sprinkle lightly with paprika and bake for 1 hour. Baste once or twice after 30 minutes. Serves 3–4.

Note: Triple this recipe for 12–14 people.

NO-KNIFE BUFFET

*Mustard-baked chicken

*Boston baked beans

*Danish meat loaf

*Old-fashioned potato salad

Tomato and purple onion salad

*Fruit salad with ginger

*Lucille Simpkin's brownies

Boston baked beans

Although Boston is credited with having originated baked beans, it actually was the Indians who soaked their beans (just as we do), then combined them with deer fat and onion in a stout clay pot and baked them overnight. The method proved to be a godsend to Pilgrim housewives because their religion forbade all worldly activities, even cooking, on Sunday. So the beans were prepared Saturday morning, cooked all day, and served hot that night, warm on Sunday. Eventually, beans became a Saturday night tradition in New England.

4	cups dry white pea beans or Great Northern beans
¾	pound salt pork
1	large onion, peeled
2	tablespoons tomato paste
2	tablespoons cider vinegar
	Powdered cloves
½	cup dark molasses
2	teaspoons salt
1	generous teaspoon freshly ground black pepper
1	cup dark brown sugar

Soak the beans overnight in enough cold water to cover them generously. Drain, put in a large kettle, and cover with fresh water by 2 inches. Bring to a boil slowly, reduce heat to simmer, and cook gently until the beans are almost tender. If the water boils away, add more boiling water to keep them well covered. Drain, saving the cooking water.

Meanwhile, scald the pork in boiling water. Cut half of it into pieces about 1-inch square, leaving the other half whole.

In the bottom of a large earthenware casserole or bean pot with a lid, place the onion. Add half the drained beans, then the cubes of pork and top with the remaining beans. Put the chunk of pork on top. Mix together the tomato paste, vinegar, a good pinch of cloves, molasses, salt, pepper, and sugar and pour over the beans. Heat 2 cups of the remaining bean liquid and pour it over all. Cover and bake in a preheated 250° oven for 6–8 hours. Keep an eye on the beans. If the liquid boils away, add any remaining bean liquid, heated to the boiling point, or boiling water. The beans should always be covered with liquid.

During the last hour of cooking, uncover the pot and allow beans to finish cooking. Do not add any more liquid during this time. Serve with steamed Boston brown bread (canned) or hot rolls. Serves 12–14.

Danish meat loaf

1	pound top round, ground twice
1	pound veal, ground twice
½	pound pork, ground twice
1	cup fresh bread crumbs soaked in 1½ cups milk
2	eggs
1	medium onion, grated
1	heaping tablespoon flour
	Salt, freshly ground pepper
3	strips bacon
	Tomato juice or chicken broth

Preheat oven to 350°.

Mix meat, soaked bread crumbs, eggs, onion, and flour together with the hands. Beat with a wooden spoon until mixture appears light and frothy. Add salt and pepper to taste. Form a loaf of the mixture in a baking dish. Put the bacon on top, and bake for about 1½ hours. Baste several times during baking with the juice or stock.

Slice thin when cool. Serves 8–10 as part of a buffet. Double (making 2 loaves) for 16.

Old-fashioned potato salad

```
5       pounds boiling potatoes
1       large onion
½       green pepper, chopped
2       cups chopped celery
6       hard-cooked eggs, cut in eighths
½–¾ cup pickle relish
¾       cup mayonnaise
¼       cup vinegar
```

Put potatoes in a large pot and cover with cold water. Bring to a boil and cook until tender but do not overcook. When cool enough to handle, but still warm, peel and cut into cubes about 1-inch square. Grate onion over potatoes. Add green pepper, celery, hard-cooked eggs, and relish and toss gently with a wooden spoon. Mix vinegar with mayonnaise to make a smooth sauce and pour over. Mix again gently but thoroughly. Serves 12–14.

Fruit salad with ginger

DRESSING:
```
1       lemon
1       lime
1       orange
5–6     slices crystallized ginger
1½      cups sugar
¾       cups cold water
¼       teaspoon cream of tartar
```

68   DINNERS

Remove zest (colored skin) of lemon, orange, and lime in thin strips, using a potato peeler. Do not take off any of the white pith. Julienne the zest. Set aside these three fruits; they will not be used in this recipe.

Wash the sugar crystals off the ginger and cut in slivers. Put ginger slivers and and julienned zest in a saucepan. Cover with cold water, bring to a boil, and simmer 5 to 7 minutes. Pour into a strainer and rinse with cold water.

Combine sugar, water, and cream of tartar in a saucepan. Bring to a boil and stir until sugar dissolves and syrup is clear. Add the zest mixture. Bring to a second boil and simmer 5 minutes. Cool and refrigerate until ready to use. Makes enough syrup for about 10 cups of fruit.

THE FRUIT:
      fresh blueberries
      cantaloupe balls
      honeydew balls
      canned mandarin oranges
      peeled seedless grapes
      grapefruit slices
      strawberries
      pitted cheeries

Combine any or all of the above, plus any other fruit desired, in any quantity or proportions. Avoid watermelon, however, as it gives off too much water. An hour or so before serving, pour the dressing over the fruit. Serve very cold in a bowl or, for a more elaborate presentation, in a hollowed-out watermelon basket, and garnish with mint leaves. Allow about 10 cups of fruit for 12–14 people.

Lucille Simpkin's brownies

½ pound butter
3 ounces unsweetened chocolate
½ cup flour
1 cup sugar
3 eggs
2 teaspoons vanilla extract
½ cup coarsely chopped walnuts (optional)
   Butter for pan
   Confectioner's sugar

Preheat oven to 350°.

Melt butter and chocolate together. Allow to cool.

Mix together flour and sugar.

Pour cooled chocolate mixture over flour mixture, beat in eggs one at a time, until fudgy and shiny. Add vanilla. Add nuts if desired.

Butter a 9-inch square pan and pour in batter. Bake for 20–25 minutes. Cut into squares while hot, then allow to cool in pan. Sprinkle with confectioner's sugar when cool. Makes 16 brownies.

Shrimp curry

½   cup finely chopped onion
2   cloves garlic, minced
4   tablespoons butter
¼   cup flour
2   tablespoons curry powder, or ιo taste
½   teaspoon ground ginger
1   teaspoon salt
2   cups chicken broth or bouillon
1   cup light cream
3   cups cooked peeled shrimp (1½ pounds uncooked small shrimp)
2   tablespoons lemon juice
    Cayenne pepper (optional)

Sauté onion and garlic in butter over low heat until wilted. Stir in flour, curry powder, ginger, and salt; add chicken broth and cream, blend, and cook until thickened, stirring occasionally.

Add shrimp and lemon juice and continue cooking until shrimp are hot. Do not allow to boil. Correct seasonings and add more curry powder, or cayenne pepper if you like it hot.

Serve over hot cooked rice with any or all of the garnishes. Serves 4 as a main course, 6–8 as a buffet dish.

Chicken curry

Use the preceding recipe for shrimp curry, substituting 3 cups cooked diced chicken for the shrimp. Add ¼ teaspoon cayenne and 1 tablespoon turmeric when you add the curry powder.

CURRY BUFFET FOR A CROWD

*Shrimp curry

*Chicken curry

Saffron rice

*Curry garnishes

*Plain and chili papadums

Sugared fresh sliced mangoes and strawberries in cream

Curry garnishes

Provide the following garnishes in individual bowls, a spoon to each.

Chopped roasted salted peanuts
Raisins (plumped in sherry and drained)
Fresh lemon quarters
Mango pickle
Bananas, diced
Apples, diced, unpeeled
Crumbled bacon
Chutney
Cucumbers in yogurt
Chopped egg yolk
Chopped egg white
Spiced lemon pickle

Note: Special items such as mango and spiced lemon pickle and papadums can be purchased in shops dealing in exotic foods and spices.

Papadums

Papadums are one of the many interesting Indian flat breads that can now be enjoyed at home. Made of lentil flour, they are available plain and spiced with chili or, for the very adventurous, with black pepper. They are perfect with curried dishes and also make an interesting accompaniment to cocktails. Traditionally they are deep-fried in oil (in which case they must be watched carefully, turned at the first sign of puffing, and removed before becoming brown). An alternative and much easier method is to hold each papadum over a gas flame until it puffs and blisters slightly and becomes crisp and crunchy. Serve while still crisp in a large basket lined with a napkin.

Chicken cutlets parmigiana

2	tablespoons flour
¾	teaspoon salt
¼	teaspoon freshly ground pepper
4	chicken breasts, boned and skinned
3	tablespoons olive oil, or half oil, half butter
1	clove garlic, minced
	Oregano
1	15-ounce jar marinara sauce or 2 cups fresh tomato sauce
6	ounces mozzarella cheese in thin slices
4	tablespoons grated Parmesan cheese
2	tablespoons melted butter

Put flour, salt, and pepper in a plastic bag and shake chicken breasts in it to coat, then heat oil and sauté chicken until pale golden—about 3–5 minutes on each side. Remove, and keep warm. Add marinara sauce, garlic, and a good pinch of oregano to skillet, and bring to a simmer. Add cutlets, place mozzarella on top, sprinkle with Parmesan and drizzle the melted butter over. Cover and cook 8–10 minutes on moderate heat or until cheese melts. Serves 4.

EASY ITALIAN DINNER I

*Chicken cutlets parmigiana

*Garlic bread

Green salad

Fresh fruit and *Sesame seed cookies

Garlic bread

½ cup butter, softened
2   cloves garlic, put through a press
1   loaf Italian or French bread

Preheat oven to 375°.

Cream the butter with the garlic and blend well. Slice the bread slightly on the diagonal, but do not cut all the way through. Spread one side of each slice generously with the garlic mixture. Wrap in foil and bake for 10 minutes. Open foil and bake 10 minutes longer to brown slightly.

Herbed garlic bread

To make herbed garlic bread, cream the butter and garlic, beat in 1 tablespoon lemon juice, drop by drop. Blend in ¼ teaspoon oregano, ¼ teaspoon chopped chives, and 2 tablespoons chopped fresh parsley. Season with salt and pepper. Spread the mixture lavishly on each slice of bread and bake as above.

Sesame seed cookies

¼	pound unsalted butter
2	cups light brown sugar
1	egg
½	teaspoon baking powder
¼	teaspoon salt
1	cup flour
1	teaspoon vanilla
¾	cup toasted sesame seeds (benne seeds) (see note)
	Butter for baking sheet

Preheat oven to 325°.

Cream the butter with the sugar until light and fluffy. Beat egg and add to butter mixture. Stir baking powder and salt into flour and blend in. Stir in vanilla and sesame seeds. Butter a cookie sheet and drop batter by spoonfuls onto it. Bake until golden brown—about 10 minutes. Cool 1 minute on sheet and remove. Makes about 4 dozen.

Note: To toast sesame seeds: Put in an ungreased skillet over moderate heat, shaking pan occasionally until seeds become golden and begin to "pop."

Roasted marinated peppers

6   medium green and/or red peppers
      Garlic dressing (see recipe below)

Preheat oven to 475°.

Wash peppers. Place directly on oven rack and roast 10–15 minutes, turning 2–3 times. Increase oven heat to BROIL—turn peppers and cook 15 minutes longer or until the skins are black.

Place peppers in a brown paper bag, close top, and cool peppers until they can be handled. Remove the blackened peel with a sharp knife, then halve, core and seed peppers. Put them in a shallow, wide glass or porcelain baking dish, pour over dressing, and marinate overnight. Serve or store in jar in the refrigerator.

Garlic dressing

½   cup good olive oil
½   teaspoon oregano
2   garlic cloves, crushed
1   teaspoon salt
    Several grindings of black pepper

Combine all ingredients and mix well.

Sea bass marechiare

2   cloves garlic, crushed
¼   cup olive oil
2   sea bass, 1½–2 pounds, boned with heads removed
¼   cup clam juice, chicken broth or fish stock
      Salt, freshly ground pepper
1   cup fresh Tomato Sauce (see Index)
      Chopped parsley

Sauté garlic in olive oil until golden. Discard garlic. Dry fish on paper towels and season with salt and pepper. Sauté briefly on both sides in the oil over fairly high heat until golden. Remove fish from pan and keep warm.

Add clam juice or chicken broth, scrape up any brown bits, bring to the boil, and reduce by half. Add tomato sauce; season to taste.

Return the fish to the pan and cook gently, covered, 10–15 minutes.

If the sauce in the pan seems too thin, uncover for last few minutes of cooking and raise heat. Serve on a heated platter, liberally sprinkled with parsley. Serves 4.

Chick-peas and rice

1   can chick-peas, drained and rinsed
2   cloves garlic
3   tablespoons olive oil
1–1½ cups rice (not instant), cooked in chicken broth
       Salt, freshly ground pepper

Put garlic through a press or mince it and sauté gently in olive oil until pale gold. Add chick-peas and sauté 8–10 minutes. Mix with warm cooked rice. Add salt and pepper to taste. Turn into a warm bowl and serve. Serves 4–6.

Fruits in Spumante

This is a refreshing, easy dish that may be prepared early in the day. Combine seasonal fruits, such as peaches and berries or a combination of berries, nectarines, navel orange slices, and strawberries—whatever you like that is in season. Use enough to yield 4–5 cups of fruit. (Don't, however, use melon, as it gives off too much liquid.) Wash and dry fruit (except raspberries or blackberries, if used), remove stems, and cut fruit up attractively—pears, nectarines, and peaches in nice wedges; large strawberries halved; skin and pith (core) removed from oranges and sliced nicely. Remove pits from cherries, if used. Place in serving bowl and refrigerate if preparing ahead, but bring to room temperature before serving. Pour ¾ bottle of chilled spumante (a slightly sweet Italian sparkling white wine) over the fruit. Serves 6.

Flounder with scallions

1 pound flounder fillets
¼ cup cornstarch
1 egg white
2 tablespoons dry sherry
¼ teaspoon ground ginger
Freshly ground black pepper to taste
3 tablespoons vegetable oil
1 cup thinly sliced fresh mushrooms
1 cup chopped scallions, white and part of the green
1 tablespoon soy sauce

Cut fish into uniform 1- × 2-inch pieces. Dry fish pieces.

Put cornstarch on a plate. Combine egg white, 1 table-spoon of the sherry, and ginger and pepper in a small bowl. Dip fish first in cornstarch to coat thoroughly, then in egg white mixture.

Heat oil in a wok or large skillet. When oil is very hot, add coated fish pieces and fry them quickly until they are golden brown on both sides. (Keep them moving and turn them over as they cook.) Remove fish to a warm serving dish. Add mushrooms and scallions to wok or skillet and stir-fry a minute or two. Add remaining 1 tablespoon of sherry and soy sauce, stir and pour contents of pan over fish. Serve at once. Serves 2–4 (depending on whether it is the main course or part of an oriental meal).

ORIENTAL-STYLE DINNER

*Flounder with scallions

*Sweet-and-pungent shrimp

*Beef, cauliflower, and snow peas

Steamed rice

*Baked bananas with rum

Sweet-and-pungent shrimp

¼ cup brown sugar
2 tablespoons cornstarch
½ teaspoon salt
¼ cup vinegar
1 tablespoon soy sauce
¼ teaspoon ground ginger
1 20-ounce can pineapple chunks, drained (reserve juice)
1 green pepper, seeded and cut into thin strips
2 small onions, cut in thin rings
1 pound shrimp, cooked and peeled

Mix sugar, cornstarch, and salt in a saucepan. Add vinegar, soy sauce, ginger, and juice drained from pineapple.

Cook slowly until slightly thickened, stirring constantly. Add green pepper, onion, and pineapple. Simmer 2 minutes. Add shrimp and bring to a boil. Serve immediately with hot rice. Serves 4.

Beef, cauliflower, and snow peas

1	pound flank steak, very thinly sliced on the diagonal (it is easiest to do this if meat is partially frozen)
1	tablespoon cornstarch
¼	cup soy sauce
1	cup chicken broth or stock
2	tablespoons vegetable oil
2	cloves garlic, minced
¼	cup chopped onion
2	teaspoons salt
	Freshly ground pepper
½	medium head cauliflower, broken into florets
¼	pound snow peas, stems removed

Cut steak into 2-inch strips; mix cornstarch and soy sauce and set aside. Heat chicken stock and set aside.

Heat oil in heavy skillet or wok until very hot. Add garlic and cook for 2–3 minutes. Add beef and sauté quickly, keeping it moving, just until it loses color, about 30 seconds.

Add onion, salt, and pepper to taste, stirring constantly for another half minute or so. Add chicken broth, bring quickly to the boil, then add cauliflower pieces, a few at a time. Cook 3 minutes, then add snow peas, stirring constantly, for another few minutes. After 7 minutes maximum, cauliflower should be tender and pea pods a bright green. Add soy sauce mixture, mix thoroughly, and stir until thickened. Turn into a serving dish and serve immediately. Serves 4 as a main course, 6–8 as part of an oriental meal.

Baked bananas with rum

```
        Butter for dish
6       bananas, ripe but not overripe
½       cup light brown sugar
3       tablespoons water
        Juice of 1 lemon
3       tablespoons butter
½       cup rum
        Heavy cream
```

Preheat oven to 400°.

Butter an ovenproof dish, large enough to hold bananas.

Peel bananas, slice in half lengthwise, and put in prepared dish.

Dissolve the sugar in the water in a small saucepan, over moderate heat. Add the lemon juice, stir, and pour over bananas. Dot with butter. Bake for 15 minutes, pour rum over, and bake 15 minutes more. Baste 2 or 3 times. Serve warm on warm plates with heavy cream. Serves 6.

Artichokes vinaigrette

Choose plump artichokes without brown spots. Trim prickles off with a scissors and slice off stem evenly so it can stand upright. If you wish, remove choke by gently spreading apart leaves and scooping around and out with a long-handled spoon.

Bring 6 quarts of water to a boil, add 3 tablespoons salt, and cook uncovered for about 15 minutes (20 minutes if choke has not been removed).

Place upside down briefly to drain and serve at room temperature with herbed sauce vinaigrette (see p. 238).

WINTER DINNER

*Artichokes vinaigrette

*Baked lamb shanks

*Armenian rice pilaff
with noodles

Green salad

Cheese

*Oranges orientale

*Almond crescent
cookies (Kourabiedes)

Baked lamb shanks

4	large or 6 small lamb shanks
	Salt, freshly ground pepper
2	cloves garlic, finely minced
1	teaspoon thyme
2	small carrots, cut in thin 2-inch strips
2	medium onions, thinly sliced
2	ribs celery, cut in thin 2-inch strips
2	bay leaves, crumbled
1	cup tomato sauce
½	cup dry white wine
½	cup water
¼	cup olive oil

Preheat oven to 275°.

Mix salt and pepper to taste, garlic, and thyme and rub into the lamb shanks.

Sprinkle the bottom of a roasting pan large enough to hold the shanks with the carrots, onions, celery, and bay leaves. Arrange the shanks on top and mix the tomato sauce, wine, water, and olive oil and pour over lamb shanks. Cover tightly and bake for 1½–2 hours, depending on the size of the shanks. Meat should be fork-tender at the end.

During the last half hour of cooking raise the oven temperature to 400° and uncover the roasting pan. Baste the shanks frequently.

When the shanks are done, remove them to a large heated platter and keep warm. Put the sauce and the vegetables through a food mill or push through a sieve. Correct the seasoning, skim the fat, and serve in a heated sauceboat with shanks. Serves 4–6.

Armenian rice pilaff with noodles

2   tablespoons vegetable oil
½   cup very fine egg noodles
2   cups long-grain rice
¼   pound butter
3   cups chicken broth, boiling
1   cup boiling water
      Salt, freshly ground pepper

Preheat oven to 300°.

Heat oil in a heavy ovenproof casserole. Add noodles and cook over medium heat, stirring constantly with a wooden spoon, until noodles are golden brown.

Add rice, butter, chicken broth, water, and salt and pepper to taste. Stir over low heat until butter has melted. Cover and bake 25–30 minutes in a 300° oven or until the liquid has been absorbed.

Remove from oven, put a folded tea towel between the lid and the pot, and let sit 10–15 minutes before serving. (This ensures dry, fluffy rice.) Serves 4–6.

Oranges orientale

4–6 fine oranges, preferably navels or temples
½   cup water
1½ cups granulated sugar
¼   cup orange juice
¼   cup Grand Marnier or Cointreau

Remove the zest, or colored part of the skin of the oranges, using a potato peeler so as not to pick up any of the white; cut in long strips if possible. Then julienne the strips into thin slivers. Set oranges aside.

Put julienned peel in a small saucepan. Cover with cold water, bring to a boil, and simmer for 5 minutes. Drain in a strainer and run cold water over the peel. Again put the peel in the saucepan, cover with water, and repeat the process. Drain.

In another saucepan, heat the water and sugar, stirring until sugar dissolves; boil gently until it reaches the soft-ball stage—230° on a candy thermometer. Immediately remove from heat and gently stir in peel. Let peel stand in syrup for 30 minutes. Add the orange juice and the Grand Marnier to the syrup after the 30 minutes.

Meanwhile, carefully remove the white pith from the peeled oranges with a very sharp knife. Slice them thin and arrange in a serving dish. Pour the syrup over oranges, chill and serve.

Note: This dish can be prepared several hours ahead and refrigerated, covered with plastic wrap, until serving time. Serves 4–6.

Almond crescent cookies

(Kourabiedes)

1	pound unsalted butter
½	cup sugar
2	eggs yolks, lightly beaten
⅔	cup finely chopped blanched almonds
2	tablespoons Cognac or other brandy
4½	cups flour, sifted
1	teaspoon baking powder
¼	teaspoon salt
	Butter for baking sheets
	Confectioner's sugar for dusting

Cream butter and sugar until fluffy and light. Beat in yolks, almonds, and Cognac. Resift flour with baking powder and salt. Work the flour mixture into butter mixture. Knead briefly; dough will be stiff.

Roll into long ½-inch-thick sausage shapes and chill 30 minutes.

Preheat oven to 400°. Butter baking sheets. Cut dough into 2-inch pieces and shape into crescents on the baking sheets. Bake for 20 minutes or until very lightly browned.

Sift confectioner's sugar onto a large sheet of foil or waxed paper. Upon removing cookies from the oven put each on sugar, sift additional sugar generously over tops and sides. Cool completely before putting into airtight tins. Makes about 5 dozen cookies.

Hot glazed corned beef

5	pounds corned beef brisket
3	large onions, sliced
2–3	cloves garlic, minced
6	cloves
3	bay leaves
1	tablespoon Dusseldorf or other sweet mustard
⅓	cup light brown sugar

Put beef in a Dutch oven or other heavy ovenproof casserole with a lid. Cover with cold water. Bring to the boil. Discard water and repeat, adding onions, garlic, cloves, and bay leaves. Cover pot with aluminum foil securely and put lid on top. Simmer gently, allowing 50 minutes per pound cooking time.

Preheat oven to 350°. Remove meat from pot, drain, and place in a shallow pan, fat side up. Score fat as you would a ham, spread on mustard, then sugar.

Bake 15–20 minutes or until well glazed. Serves 6–8.

COLD-WEATHER TRAVELER

*Hot glazed corned beef

*Potato ragout

Endive and watercress salad

*Apple crisp with cream

Potato ragout

½ pound sliced bacon, cut into ½-inch strips
2 large onions, coarsely chopped
1 clove garlic, minced
3 pounds potatoes, peeled and cut in 1-inch cubes
1 cup chicken stock
1 tablespoon fresh tarragon or ½ teaspoon dried
    Salt, freshly ground pepper
2 tablespoons wine vinegar
1 tablespoon olive oil
    Chopped parsley

Put the bacon in a saucepan, cover it with cold water, and bring to the boil. Drain bacon and dry on paper towels.

Sauté bacon in a heavy skillet for 3–5 minutes. Remove all but 2 tablespoons of the fat and add the onions and garlic. Cook until the onions are transparent.

Add potatoes, stock, tarragon, and salt and pepper to taste. Cover and simmer 15 minutes or until the potatoes are tender but not mushy and the liquid is absorbed.

Add vinegar and oil and toss lightly. Sprinkle with the parsley and serve hot. Serves 6–8.

Apple crisp

Butter for baking dish
4 cups peeled tart apple slices (7–8 medium apples)
1 cup light brown sugar
1 teaspoon cinnamon
½ teaspoon nutmeg
1 tablespoon lemon juice
2 tablespoons orange juice
Grated zest (colored skin) of 1 orange
¾ cup flour
Salt
4 tablespoons butter

Preheat oven to 375°.

Butter a 1-quart baking dish or 9-inch Pyrex dish. Arrange slices in dish. Mix ½ cup brown sugar with cinnamon and nutmeg and sprinkle over apples. Add juices and zest.

To make crumb topping, mix the remaining sugar with the flour and a dash of salt and cut in butter. Sprinkle over apple slices and bake 35–40 minutes or until apples are tender and the top browned. Serve warm with cold heavy cream. Serves 6.

Note: Can be made ahead and gently warmed in oven before serving.

Boiled beef and chicken...

4	pounds short ribs of beef
1	onion, peeled
2	stalks celery
2	carrots
3	cloves garlic
1½	tablespoons salt
1	chicken, cut up

Put meat in a deep heavy pot with the onion, celery, carrots, and garlic. Cover with cold water and bring to a boil. Boil for 5 minutes and skim off any scum that appears. Cover and simmer for ½ hour. Add chicken and continue cooking another half hour.

Serve meat and cut up chicken together with boiled potatoes and horseradish sauce passed separately.

Note: Potatoes may be boiled in the same pot with the meat if desired. Serves 4.

...with horseradish sauce

2	tablespoons butter
2	tablespoons flour
1	cup hot broth from boiled beef
2	tablespoons freshly grated horseradish or 4-ounce jar prepared horseradish
2	tablespoons heavy cream
1	teaspoon sugar
1	tablespoon Dijon-type mustard
	Salt
	Vinegar (see note)

DINNERS   89

FAMILY WINTER DINNER

*Boiled beef and chicken with horseradish sauce

Boiled potatoes

Beets in butter and coarse salt

Sour pickles

Mustard

Green salad

*Gingerbread cake

Make a roux by melting butter over low heat, then stirring in flour. Cook for a few minutes, then stir in hot beef broth. Cook and stir sauce until smooth and thickened. Remove from heat and stir in horseradish, cream, sugar, and mustard. Season with salt and vinegar to taste (see note).

Reheat but do not boil.

Note: As prepared horseradish contains vinegar, the kind of horseradish you use will determine the amount of vinegar needed.

Gingerbread cake

½ cup light brown sugar, firmly packed
3 ounces butter, at room temperature
½ cup molasses
½ cup sour cream
1 egg, lightly beaten
1 cup flour
1 teaspoon ground ginger
1 teaspoon cinnamon
1 teaspoon baking soda dissolved in a little warm water
   Salt
¼ cup seedless raisins
¼ cup chopped pecans or walnuts
¼ cup chopped candied ginger
   Butter and flour for pan

Preheat oven to 350°.

Cream butter and sugar together until fluffy. Beat in molasses and sour cream. Beat in eggs. Stir in flour, ginger, cinnamon, baking soda, and a pinch of salt, then fold in raisins, nuts, and ginger. Butter and flour an 8-inch square pan, pour in batter and bake for about 45 minutes. Do not open oven door until cake starts to pull away from the sides of pan. Cake is done when tester comes out clean.

Cut cake in squares when slightly cooled off but still warm. Serve warm with whipped cream, applesauce or Sabayon sauce (see Index), or you can pass all three sauces and let the diner decide. Serves 8–10.

Note: This recipe may be doubled. Use a 10- × 14- × 12-inch pan and bake 50–55 minutes.

Alsatian cabbage and potatoes

4–5	medium potatoes
1	large head green cabbage
1	large onion, chopped
	Cooking oil or rendered chicken or goose fat
	Salt, freshly ground pepper

Peel potatoes and cut into manageable halves or quarters. Wash cabbage, drain and quarter. Put potatoes in salted water to cover. Place the cabbage quarters on top. Bring to the boil. Cover and cook until potatoes are just tender. Do not overcook.

Remove cabbage and drain. Chop coarsely and set aside. Drain potatoes and mash coarsely with a potato masher. (Do not puree or dish will not have proper texture.) Set aside.

Sauté the onion in 4 tablespoons oil until golden brown; add cabbage and continue sautéing 3–4 minutes. Add the cabbage-onion mixture to the mashed potatoes, mixing thoroughly, and season to taste with salt and pepper. Reheat briefly and serve. Serves 6.

Note: These proportions are rough. The size of the cabbage, the potatoes, etc. almost doesn't matter.

This dish is traditionally served with hot sausages but we find it equally good with hot tongue or corned beef.

SNOWY-DAY DINNER

*Cream of tomato soup (see p. 20)

*Alsatian cabbage and potatoes

Assortment of mustards

*Hot smoked tongue

*Applecake with whipped cream

Hot smoked tongue

1	smoked beef tongue, about 4 pounds
1	onion stuck with 2 cloves
1	bay leaf
2	cloves garlic
3	sprigs parsley

Put tongue in a large pot and cover with cold water. Bring to a boil, and boil for 5 minutes. Remove any scum that appears. Add onion, bay leaf, garlic, and parsley. Cover tightly, lower heat and simmer gently until tender, about 50 minutes per pound.

When done, remove from broth, skin carefully, and return to broth to keep warm. Slice before serving.

Serves 6.

Applecake with whipped cream

	Butter and flour for pan
3	eggs
2	cups sugar
½	cup vegetable oil
3	cups flour
1	teaspoon baking soda
	Salt
1	teaspoon cinnamon
3	cups peeled and coarsely chopped apples
1	cup chopped pecans
2	teaspoons vanilla
¼	pound butter
1	cup light brown sugar
½	cup milk
	Whipped cream

Preheat oven to 325°.

Butter and flour a 10-inch tube pan.

Beat the eggs with the sugar until they are thick and form a ribbon when a spoonful is lifted and dribbled onto the surface. Add vegetable oil and beat until blended. Stir in flour, soda, 1 teaspoon salt, and cinnamon and blend well.

Stir in apples, pecans, and vanilla and mix well. Turn batter into prepared pan. Bake 1 hour and 15 minutes, or until cake tests clean.

Make topping: Melt butter in a saucepan, add brown sugar, milk, and a pinch of salt and boil for 3 minutes.

When cake is done, cool for 5 minutes in pan, then turn out onto serving platter. Prick a number of holes over surface of cake, using a skewer or a toothpick and while both are still warm, pour topping over cake. Serve with whipped cream.

Risotto

¼–½ cup butter
½   cup minced onion
2   cups Arborio Italian rice (see Index)
1   scant cup dry white wine
4–5   cups hot chicken broth
2   tablespoons butter
    Freshly grated Parmesan cheese

Heat butter in heavy saucepan and cook onion gently until pale golden. Add rice and stir constantly until opaque, about 5 minutes. Stir in wine and when it is absorbed, add hot broth, ½ cup at a time as it is absorbed, always stirring. In about 20 minutes or when done, stir in butter and ½ cup cheese and serve at once, with more cheese alongside. Serves 4–6.

SATISFYING
MEATLESS
DINNER

*Risotto

*Eggplant orientale

*Buttered zucchini

*Blueberry slump

Eggplant orientale

3	medium-size eggplants
	Butter for pan
2	large yellow onions, thinly sliced
2	cloves garlic
⅓	cup oil (see note)
1	teaspoon coarse salt
	Freshly ground black pepper
	Wine vinegar
¼	cup roughly chopped fresh dill

Preheat oven to 450°.

Cut eggplant into ½-inch slices. Generously butter a rimmed cookie sheet or a large shallow baking pan. Arrange a layer of eggplant slices on it. Cover with a layer of onion (if necessary, use two pans—eggplant slices should be in one layer). Put garlic through a press, or mince, and spread on top. Drizzle oil over all. Season well with salt and pepper.

Bake in the oven for about 35 minutes or until the eggplant is tender and browned.

Let cool slightly. Chop into fine dice. Add a dash of vinegar and correct seasoning if necessary. Garnish with fresh dill. Serves 4.

Note: Use a mixture of ½ olive oil and ½ vegetable oil.

Buttered zucchini

4	medium zucchini (6–7 inches long)
⅓–½	cup chicken broth
3	tablespoons butter
	Salt, freshly ground black pepper

94   DINNERS

Wash zucchini and remove stem and blossom ends. Cut in chunky rounds, about 2 inches long. Put in saucepan with broth and bring to a boil. Cover and cook about 7 minutes, until tender but firm. Uncover and boil off liquid for a few minutes if necessary. Drop in butter and shake pot gently until it melts. Season with salt and pepper and serve immediately. Serves 4.

Blueberry slump

2	pint boxes blueberries, picked over, or 2 packages frozen blueberries, slightly defrosted
¾	cup sugar
2	tablespoons cornstarch
	Grated zest (colored skin) of 1 orange

BATTER:

½	cup sugar
4	tablespoons butter
	Dash salt
1	egg, lightly beaten
½	cup milk
1½	cups sifted cake flour
2	teaspoons baking powder

Preheat the oven to 425°. Butter a 9- × 12-inch Pyrex baking dish.

Pick over the berries, wash, and dry. Mix together the sugar and cornstarch and orange rind, toss with the berries, and put in baking dish.

Cream together the butter and sugar, add a dash of salt, and blend in egg. Add milk and mix in well. Stir in flour and baking powder, beat briefly and briskly to make a thick, soft batter; spoon over the berries, leaving about a one-inch border of berries visible (batter spreads). Bake in the preheated oven for 20 to 25 minutes, or until top is dappled with gold. Serve warm with vanilla ice cream if desired. Serves 6–8.

CHILI BUFFET

*Guacamole with taco chips (see p. 183)

*Chili

Hot rice

Salad of mixed lettuces, radishes, and avocado wedges

*Gladys's flan

Chili

3	pounds beef chuck, ground
3	medium onions, chopped
1	green pepper, chopped
3–4	cloves garlic
½	teaspoon oregano
½	teaspoon cumin seed (see note) or ½ teaspoon ground cumin
1	small can tomato paste
1	can whole tomatoes (2 pounds), chopped
3	tablespoons good chili powder
2	fifteen-ounce cans red kidney beans, drained
	Salt and fresh pepper

Brown the meat in a heavy stew pot. Add onions, pepper, garlic, oregano, and cumin. Mix well. Add tomatoes and tomato paste, and about 1 quart water. Salt liberally, add several good grindings of pepper and the chili powder (since this is a personal taste, you may wish to add more chili powder later for a more pronounced flavor). Simmer for 1½ hours, then add the beans. Simmer another half hour. Taste, correct seasonings, and when it tastes right let it sit around for several hours for the flavor to ripen.

It should be made at least one day ahead, but two or three are even better. Serves 8.

Note: If using cumin seed, roast briefly in an ungreased skillet until brown and then crush with a rolling pin to release flavor.

Gladys's Flan

This is a Latin version of the classic crème caramel in which low baking heat and the most gentle beating of the eggs yield an incredibly smooth, velvety, yet firm custard that cuts almost like cake. Instead of the caramel coating it is dressed with a raspberry sauce after unmolding.

	Butter for mold
1	can sweetened condensed milk
2	cans evaporated milk
4	cups regular milk
1	cup sugar
1	scraped vanilla bean
12	eggs
2	tablespoons brandy
	Raspberry sauce (see p. 14), chilled

Preheat oven to 250°.

Butter a 3-quart mold.

Combine all the milks in a saucepan, add the sugar and scraped vanilla bean, and heat gently, stirring until sugar dissolves.

Break eggs into a bowl and whisk gently. Warm eggs with a small amount of hot milk mixture added in droplets. Slowly add balance of milk mixture, whisking gently. Stir in brandy, strain into buttered mold, put mold in a pan which should be filled with enough hot water to come halfway up sides of pan. Bake for 3 hours.

Pour raspberry sauce over unmolded flan. Serves 8–10.

Note: This recipe can be halved. Reduce baking time to 2 hours.

Baked scallops in white wine

EARLY SPRING DINNER

*Baked scallops in white wine

*Roast beef

*Yorkshire pudding

*Parsnips puree

Spinach salad with garlic vinaigrette (see p. 10)

*Rum cream pie

1	cup dry white wine
½	teaspoon salt
	Freshly ground pepper
1	clove garlic, minced
2	tablespoons minced shallots
1	pint fresh scallops, washed
½	pound fresh mushrooms, sliced
3	tablespoons butter
2	tablespoons flour
1	egg yolk, beaten
	Cayenne pepper
¼	cup grated Parmesan cheese
1	tablespoon butter

Combine wine, salt, pepper, garlic, and shallots and simmer for 5 minutes. Add scallops and mushrooms, and enough water to just cover. Bring to a boil, cover, lower heat, and simmer for 5 minutes. Drain scallops and reserve liquid, keeping it warm.

Melt butter, blend in flour. Bring reserved liquid to a boil and, off heat, stir it into butter mixture. Beat a spoonful or two of the hot sauce into the beaten egg yolk, then add this to balance of sauce. Season to taste with salt, pepper, and a dash of cayenne.

Combine the scallops and mushrooms with the sauce. Divide between 6 scallop shells or pour into a small (2-cup) gratin dish. Sprinkle with cheese, dot with butter, and put in the top of a 425° oven for 10 minutes. Serves 6.

Note: This dish may be prepared ahead, and refrigerated. Add the cheese-butter topping and bake at the last minute.

Roast beef

There are several good ways to make rare juicy roast beef. Many swear by this method, developed by Anne Serrane, a well-known food writer.

1   standing rib roast, 2 to 4 ribs
     flour
     salt and pepper

Remove roast from refrigerator and allow to come to room temperature (about 4 hours before beginning to cook).

Preheat oven to 500°.

Place roast in an open shallow roasting pan, fat side up. Sprinkle with a little flour and rub the flour into the fat lightly. Season with salt and pepper.

Put the roast in preheated oven and roast according to chart, timing minutes *exactly*. When cooking time is finished, turn oven off.

Do not open door at any time. Allow roast to remain in oven till oven is lukewarm, about 2 hours. Roast will keep an internal heat suitable for serving as long as 4 hours. (Yield: 2 servings per rib.)

Roasting Chart for Rib Roasts

Number of Ribs	Weight (without short ribs)	Total Roasting Time* (at 500°)
2	4½–5 lbs.	25–30 minutes
3	8–9 lbs.	40–45 minutes
4	11–12 lbs.	55–60 minutes

*Note: This works out to 15 minutes per rib, or approximately 5 minutes cooking time *per pound of your trimmed ready-to-cook roast*.

Yorkshire Pudding

This recipe first appeared in the LVIS Cookbook *for 1916 and was given by the late Mrs. W. B. Robinson. It was repeated in 1948 and again in the 70th Anniversary Book in 1965. It is the favorite Yorkshire Pudding recipe of so many East Hampton cooks that we repeated it again.*

When roasting a piece of beef (in a 375° oven), set it on a rack so the fat will drop into the pan below. Remove enough of the fat to fill a 10-inch square baking pan to a depth of ¼ inch. About ¾ hour before serving pour in a batter made as follows:

1	pint of milk
4	eggs, beaten very light
1	pinch of salt
1	cup of flour

Bake in a 350° oven.
When done, cut in pieces and serve with the roast. Serves 6–8.

Note: Pudding also can be made right in roasting pan, when beef is done. Remove roast and keep it warm while pudding bakes.

Parsnips puree

Wash and peel 2–2½ pounds parsnips. Cover with boiling salted water and cook about 20 minutes or until tender. Drain, run cold water over, and peel when cool enough to handle. Cut into chunks, discarding woody cores. Put pieces through a food mill or ricer, or puree in blender with enough cream to get the consistency of soft mashed potatoes. Season with salt, freshly ground black pepper, and a large lump of butter and puree again if necessary till smooth. Serves 4–6.

Rum cream pie

1½	teaspoons unflavored gelatin
¼	cup water
½	cup granulated sugar
⅛	teaspoon salt
2	egg yolks
¼	cup dark rum
1	cup heavy cream, whipped
8″	graham cracker crust
	Whipped cream and chocolate curls

Sprinkle gelatin over water to soften in a medium-size heavy saucepan. Beat sugar, salt, and egg yolks together in a small bowl. Add to gelatin and stir over medium heat until mixture thickens. Do not allow to boil. Remove from heat, stir in rum, and cool until mixture thickens more and begins to set. (Twenty minutes in refrigerator will speed things up.)

Fold in whipped cream and pour into crust. Chill before serving. Garnish with chocolate curls and whipped-cream ribbons if desired. Serves 6.

ONE-DISH FISH DINNER

*Baked cod with tomatoes

Arugula salad

*Pudding Toscano

Baked cod with tomatoes

½ cup olive oil
1 cup chopped onion
4 thick cod or halibut fillets (about 2 pounds)
¼ cup chopped parsley
½ teaspoon oregano
Salt, freshly ground pepper
2 cups canned plum tomatoes, drained and chopped (reserve juice)
3 large potatoes, peeled, quartered, and parboiled for 10 minutes

Preheat oven to 400°.

Pour 2 tablespoons of olive oil in a baking dish large enough to hold comfortably all the ingredients. Spread ½ of the onions in the baking dish and top with fish. Cover with remaining onion, parsley, and oregano, and season with salt and pepper. Add remaining oil and enough juice from tomatoes or water to cover fish.

Arrange potatoes around fish. Cover with tomatoes and bake uncovered in a 400° oven about 30 minutes, or until potatoes and fish are tender. Serves 4.

Pudding Toscano

¼   cup raisins
¼   cup sultanas (golden raisins)
     Sherry
2   cups ricotta cheese
½   cup ground almonds
¼   cup candied orange peel, coarsely chopped
     Grated zest (colored skin) of 1 lemon
4   eggs
½   cup sugar
1   teaspoon almond extract
     Butter for baking dish
     Vanilla sugar

Soak the raisins and sultanas in sherry for about 1 hour to plump them up. Drain.

Preheat oven to 350°.

Push the ricotta through a sieve, add the ground almonds, candied orange peel, raisins, sultanas, and lemon zest.

Beat the eggs with the sugar until light and combine well with the cheese mixture. Stir in the almond extract. Butter a 5–6-cup baking dish and bake for about 30 minutes, or until a knife or tester inserted in center comes out clean. Sprinkle with vanilla sugar. Serves 6.

Asparagus

ELEGANT SPRING
DINNER

As with corn, there are many schools of thought on cooking this favorite. This is one good way.

Select asparagus having firm stalks without ridges and with tightly closed green tips. Their thickness is a matter of personal taste, but they should be of uniform size to cook properly.

Trim or break off the cut ends. Wash under cold running water. Make bundles of 8 or 10, tying below tips and a second time around the middle. Leave one asparagus out of the bundles for testing.

Bring a large pot of salted water to the boil. Put the bundles and the "tester," in, bring to a second boil, and cook uncovered for 10 minutes (more or less according to thickness). Try the test one— asparagus should be pliable but not limp and still retain a bright green color. Drain, run cold water over to stop the cooking, untie, and return stalks to the empty pot, shaking it gently over high heat for 1 or 2 minutes to dry them.

To serve at room temperature spread on a platter to cool.

As with artichokes, we believe the unique and delicate flavor of the asparagus can be savored only when they are served as a separate course.

ELEGANT SPRING
DINNER

*Asparagus with
*Sauce mousseline
(see Index)

*Lamb chops
Provençale

Roast potatoes

*Puree of peas and
watercress

*Endive salad

*Chocolate soufflé

Lamb chops Provençale

Use double-rib baby lamb chops, 2–2½ inches thick, and have the bones frenched. Allow 2 chops per person.

Brush the chops with olive oil and spread each side with crushed garlic. Sprinkle them with lemon juice, salt, and freshly ground pepper to taste, and let them marinate 2 hours unrefrigerated. Broil in a preheated broiler 4 inches from the heat for 6 minutes per side.

Puree of Peas and watercress

2	10-ounce packages frozen green peas, partly defrosted
	Large handful of watercress, stems removed
½	cup chicken stock
	Salt
1	tablespoon butter

Break up the frozen blocks of peas and place in a large heavy saucepan with stock, salt, and butter. Cover and let boil moderately fast. When peas are almost tender (5–7 minutes) place watercress on top; cover and continue cooking 5 minutes longer or until the watercress has wilted. Then puree in a blender until very smooth and correct seasoning.

This dish may be prepared in advance and reheated before serving, in which case add an additional tablespoon of butter. Serves 6–8.

Endive salad

```
6–8    Belgian endives
1      recipe vinaigrette dressing (see p. 237)
2      tablespoons chopped parsley
```

Cut off the root ends of the endive if they are brown and remove any bruised or blackened leaves. Carefully separate the leaves of 1 endive. Put them in a mixing bowl (other than serving bowl) and moisten with a few spoonfuls of dressing. Arrange them points up around the edges of the salad bowl.

Cut the others in half and then slice them thinly the long way in a rather thick julienne. Toss with enough vinaigrette to coat them in the mixing bowl, sprinkle with the parsley, toss again, and pile into the center of the salad bowl. Serves 6.

Chocolate soufflé

```
3      tablespoons butter
3      tablespoons flour
1½     cups milk, scalded
¾      teaspoon vanilla
6      ounces (squares) unsweetened chocolate
6      tablespoons hot water
4      egg yolks, lightly beaten
       Salt
       Scant ½ cup granulated sugar
6      egg whites
       Butter for soufflé dish
       Confectioner's sugar
       Slightly sweetened whipped cream, flavored with vanilla
```

Preheat oven to 400°. Butter a 2-quart soufflé dish and place in refrigerator.

Melt butter in a heavy saucepan over moderate heat. Add flour and blend, stirring constantly. Remove from heat. Add vanilla to milk and blend into flour mixture, stirring constantly until smooth and thick. Melt chocolate in a small saucepan. Stir into milk mixture.

Still stirring, add the hot water. Then add egg yolks, a pinch of salt and sugar. Stir hard for several minutes until smooth and shiny.

Beat egg whites until stiff. Stir a couple of spoonfuls into the chocolate mixture to lighten it, then fold in balance, using a rubber spatula and a downward-cutting and folding-up-over motion.

Turn batter into prepared soufflé dish and place in oven. After 5 minutes lower heat to 350° and cook 20–25 minutes.

Sprinkle top with confectioner's sugar and serve with whipped cream. Serves 6.

Baked snapper with prosciutto

LATE SPRING DINNER

*Baked snapper with prosciutto

*Broccoli with hollandaise

Hot rice

Green salad

*Rhubarb pie

½ cup olive oil
½ cup lemon juice
¼ teaspoon oregano
¼ teaspoon basil
½ teaspoon chopped garlic
1 cup sliced onions
3 pounds red snapper (mullet or striped bass may also be used), fileted, skin on
½ cup chopped prosciutto (1 slice ¼ inch thick will yield this amount)
½ cup fresh bread crumbs
1 tablespoon chopped parsley

Mix olive oil, lemon juice, oregano, basil, garlic, and onion in a medium-size flat baking dish. Place fillets skin side up in this marinade and let soak unrefrigerated for at least 1 hour. Discard onions.

Sandwich fillets, skin side outside, with chopped prosciutto.

Bake 30 minutes in a preheated 325° oven, basting 2 or 3 times with the marinade. Spoon out some of the liquid from the pan, mix with bread crumbs and parsley to bind, and spread over top of fillets. Brown under broiler. Cut in 4 portions. Serves 4.

Broccoli with hollandaise

1 large bunch broccoli
1 cup Blender Hollandaise (see p. 239)

Cut off any woody lower portions of stems. Cut branches in halves or quarters, to make pieces of uniform size. Wash thoroughly and boil uncovered in a large amount of salted water for about 6 minutes. Stems should be tender but not limp. Drain on towel, place in a hot serving dish, and pour melted hollandaise over. Serves 4.

Rhubarb pie

2	eggs
1½	cups sugar
4	cups fresh rhubarb, cut in 1-inch pieces
1	teaspoon grated orange rind
1	recipe cream cheese pastry (see p. 233)
3	tablespoons minute tapioca
2	tablespoons butter

Preheat oven to 425°.

Beat eggs with sugar until they form a ribbon. Add rhubarb and orange rind and let stand while you make pie crust.

Roll out half the pie crust dough and fit into a 9-inch pie plate. Sprinkle tapioca on bottom, then add rhubarb mixture. Dot with butter.

Roll out the remainder, cut 1-inch strips, and make a lattice top. Crimp edges with a fork.

Bake in 425° oven for 15 minutes, then reduce oven heat to 350° and bake 30 minutes longer. Cool on a rack. Serve warm or cold. Serves 6–8.

French lamb stew

<table>
<tr><td>FRIDAY NIGHT
TRAVELER</td></tr>
</table>

	FRIDAY NIGHT TRAVELER

*French lamb stew

Warmed French
bread

Green salad

Brie

*Wine-poached pears
with sabayon sauce

4	pounds lamb stew meat (including some from the neck, shanks, and short ribs, if possible)
	Oil for cooking
1½	teaspoons salt
	Freshly ground pepper
4	tablespoons flour
3	cups beef stock or bouillon
1	cup peeled and chopped tomatoes
2	cloves garlic, minced
½	teaspoon thyme
1	bay leaf
12	small white onions, peeled
2	tablespoons butter
2	teaspoons sugar
5–7	peeled carrots
8	potatoes
1	cup fresh shelled peas or half a 10-ounce box frozen peas
	Chopped parsley

Cut lamb into large, bite-size pieces, remove excess fat but keep all bones except, of course, slivers. Dry meat with towel and brown in hot oil in a skillet, a few pieces at a time. As they are browned, remove the pieces to a large heavy casserole with a lid.

When all the pieces are browned, sprinkle with salt, pepper, and flour, and cook, uncovered, over high heat, keeping the pieces moving until all traces of flour disappear and lamb is slightly crusty.

Add the beef broth to the skillet in which you browned the meat; scrape up all the brown bits and bring to the boil. Pour into the casserole, add tomatoes, garlic, thyme, and bay leaf. Bring to a boil, lower heat, and simmer. Meat should be almost covered by the broth. Add more if it is not. Cover and cook for 45 minutes.

While lamb is cooking, prepare the vegetables. Shell the peas if you are using fresh ones. Pour boiling water over the white onions and slip off the outer skins. Make a cross in the root ends with a knife. Sear them in butter in a skillet, then turn down the heat and sauté them gently for 10 minutes, shaking the pan from time to time so they cook evenly. Sprinkle with the sugar and cook a few minutes more to glaze lightly. Set aside. Scrape the carrots and cut into finger-size pieces; peel potatoes and halve or quarter them if they are large.

After 45 minutes, taste the sauce and correct seasoning if necessary. Put all the vegetables except the peas around the meat pieces and spoon the sauce over them. Bring again to the simmer, cover and cook about an hour or until the vegetables are tender. Just before the stew is ready, blanch the peas in an uncovered pot of boiling salted water for 5 minutes. Drain and put in casserole and spoon some sauce over them. Simmer for 10 minutes more.

Sprinkle with chopped parsley at serving time. Serves 8.

Wine-poached pears...

8	firm ripe pears
3	tablespoons lemon juice
2	cups red wine
¾	cup granulated sugar
2	sticks cinnamon
6	cloves

Peel and halve pears. Remove stems and core with a grapefruit knife. Drop into a bowl of water with 1 tablespoon lemon juice to keep from discoloring.

Bring wine, remaining lemon juice, sugar, and spices to a boil in a saucepan large enough to hold all pear halves. Drain pears and put in the boiling syrup. Reduce heat so the liquid just shivers. Cook until pears are tender, about 10 minutes. Do not overcook. Remove from heat and let pears cool in syrup for 15 minutes. Remove from liquid with slotted spoon. Boil syrup down to thicken and reduce. Pour syrup over pears and serve with sabayon sauce or sweetened whipped cream. Serves 8.

... with sabayon sauce

This sauce is very simple but like hollandaise must be made with care to avoid ending up as scrambled eggs.

4	egg yolks
⅔	cup sugar
1	cup light sherry or marsala
1	tablespoon rum

Whip the egg yolks and sugar together in the top of a double boiler until mixture is light and fluffy. Put over cold water in a double boiler and set over moderate heat, whisking constantly, keeping the water just below the boiling point, until sauce becomes thick and creamy. Off heat, add the rum and sherry. Set pan in a bowl of ice and stir until cooled. Chill in refrigerator. Makes about 2 cups. Serves 6–8.

Cold curried apple soup

2   medium onions, chopped
2   tablespoons butter
6   red apples, peeled and diced
4   cups chicken broth or stock
2   tablespoons curry powder
2   tablespoon sugar
       Salt, freshly ground pepper
1   cup light cream
       Chopped parsley or watercress leaves

Sauté onions in butter until transparent; stir in apples, chicken broth, curry powder, sugar, and salt and pepper to taste. Puree in blender, adding cream according to richness desired. Correct the seasoning and chill. Serve very cold garnished with the parsley or watercress leaves. Serves 6.

Note: This soup is equally delicious served hot in the winter.

Sautéed blowfish

Old-time fishermen are usually astonished to hear of people actually eating blowfish; this odd fish that can blow or puff itself up when danger threatens was always thrown back. The edible part is, in fact, the tail and surrounding flesh, and a great delicacy it is. Also called chicken of the sea, these sweet morsels have a taste faintly reminiscent of frog's legs. There are just a few bites to each one, so allow 4 to 6 per person, depending on size and appetites.

DINNER ON THE PORCH

*Cold curried apple soup

*Sautéed blowfish

*Green beans vinaigrette

*New potatoes with mint

*Steamed blueberry pudding with hot blueberry sauce

18–24 blowfish
⅓   cup flour
      Salt, pepper
3   tablespoons olive oil
3   tablespoons butter
      Lemon wedges

Dry the fish well. Mix flour and salt and pepper to taste in a plastic or paper bag, add fish, a few at a time, and shake to coat them.

Melt 2 tablespoons butter and 2 tablespoons olive oil in a large heavy skillet. Sauté half the fish over fairly high heat, about 5 minutes per side, or until golden. Do not crowd them in the pan: it is better to cook 2 batches.

Remove first batch, keep warm, add additional butter and oil, and do second batch the same way. Serves 6.

Green beans vinaigrette

1½   pounds fresh string beans, trimmed
1   small red onion, finely minced
1   cup vinaigrette dressing (see Index)
      Salt and freshly ground black pepper

Bring a large amount of salted water to a rolling boil. Throw in the beans a handful at a time so that water does not stop boiling. Boil uncovered 3–5 minutes. Immediately run cold water in pot and drain.

Mix minced onion into vinaigrette. Pour over cooled beans, toss, and season to taste. Serves 8.

New potatoes with mint

If you can get really fresh new potatoes, scrub them and boil rapidly in salted water until tender. Drain, return to pot, and shake briefly over heat to dry them. Dress with melted butter, salt, and freshly ground pepper. Serve in a heated dish and sprinkle with a handful of chopped mint.

If the potatoes are not the freshest, or the idea of serving in the skins does not appeal, peel after boiling. The skins should slip off easily. Dress and serve as above.

Steamed blueberry pudding...

2½   cups plus 3 tablespoons flour
3½   teaspoons baking powder
⅛   teaspoon salt
¼   pound butter
1   cup granulated sugar
2   eggs, beaten
1   cup milk
    Butter for mold
2   cups blueberries
    Hot blueberry sauce (see recipe below)

Sift together 2½ cups flour, baking powder, and salt.

Cream butter and sugar well, add beaten eggs and blend well. Add flour mixture and milk alternately in small quantities, blending well after each addition.

Butter a 1½-quart pudding mold (also called a chimney mold) and pour in about ¼ of the mixture. Toss the berries with the remaining flour and fold into the remaining mixture. Pour into mold and fasten mold cover.

Put mold in a deep kettle; pour enough boiling water around it so that water level reaches ⅔ up the sides of mold, cover kettle, and steam over low heat for 1 hour and 10 minutes. Add water to kettle as needed to maintain level.

Unmold and serve with hot blueberry sauce. Serves 6.

... with hot blueberry sauce

2	cups blueberries
½	cup sugar

Crush a handful of blueberries in the bottom of a saucepan, with a fork. Add the remaining berries and sugar and simmer gently, uncovered, about 15 minutes, over gentle heat.

Let cool slightly, then process briefly in a food processor and serve warm. Makes about 2 cups.

Rice salad

3   cups hot cooked white rice (not instant)
½   cup olive oil (can be a mixture of the oil in artichoke jar and regular olive oil)
½   pound fresh mushrooms
3   tablespoons butter
1   cup sliced marinated artichoke hearts (available in jars)
1   cup fresh tomatoes, peeled, seeded, and chopped
½   cup sliced black olives
1   teaspoon freshly ground black pepper
     Salt
½   purple onion, thinly sliced

Toss hot rice with the oil in a large bowl, using 2 forks. Set aside to cool.

Slice mushrooms thinly and sauté briefly in the butter. Add to the rice with artichoke hearts, tomatoes, olives, pepper, salt to taste, and onion, and toss well again. Serve salad at room temperature. Serves 6.

Variation: If fresh tomatoes are not available, slivers of sweet red pepper, either fresh or canned, make an agreeable substitute.

PORTABLE COLD DINNER (OR LUNCH)

*Rice salad

*Cold stuffed breast of veal with
*Garlic mayonnaise (see p. 236)

*Cucumber salad (see p. 145)

Italian whole wheat bread with butter

*Stuffed peaches

Stuffed breast of veal

A whole breast of veal can weigh from 4½ to 9 pounds, depending on the size of the animal. Ask the butcher for a piece about 3½–4½ pounds with a pocket for stuffing, and to remove as many of the rib bones as possible. The amount of stuffing required will depend, of course, on the size of the breast.

1	medium onion, diced
4	tablespoons butter
1½	pounds mixed ground pork and veal
¼	cup chopped parsley
½	cup bread crumbs
	Salt, freshly ground pepper
½–1	cup dry white wine
1	breast of veal with a pocket, 3½–4½ pounds
1	clove garlic, put through a press
1	teaspoon thyme
3	tablespoons cooking oil

GRAVY:

2	tablespoons butter
2	tablespoons flour
	Chicken broth
¼	cup heavy cream

Preheat oven to 325°.

Sauté the onions in 1 tablespoon butter until wilted. Mix with the meat, parsley, and bread crumbs and season with salt and pepper to taste. Moisten with a little white wine and stuff the pocket with the mixture. (The amount it holds will depend on the size of the breast and the pocket.) Cover the open end with a double piece of aluminum foil and shape it with the hands to cover well. A couple of skewers may help to secure the opening.

Combine the garlic, 1 teaspoon salt, and thyme, and rub mixture well into the breast.

Heat remaining butter and oil and brown the breast on both sides. Then place in preheated oven for about 1 hour, or allow 20 minutes per pound, remembering that the stuffing is part of the weight. Baste occasionally with the pan juices.

If you plan to serve the veal hot, make a gravy as follows:

Remove the meat from the roaster pan and keep warm. Skim off any excess fat from the pan juices. In a saucepan melt the butter, add the flour, and stir until smoothly blended. Add pan juices and enough chicken broth to make about a cup of liquid. Correct seasoning and stir in the heavy cream.

This dish is a good traveler. Carry the meat covered in foil and the gravy in a separate jar. It can be served hot, warm, or cold. Serves 4–6.

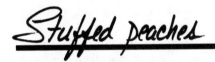

Stuffed peaches

7	medium-size ripe peaches
2	tablespoons sugar
2	tablespoons butter
5–6	crushed Amaretti macaroons
1	egg yolk
2	tablespoons heavy cream
1	tablespoon Cognac

Preheat oven to 350°. Butter a baking dish.

Peel one peach. Cut flesh in pieces. Cut remaining peaches in half. Remove pits and scoop out a bit of the pulp from each half. Combine pulp with cut-up peach and mash well with a fork. Add butter and crushed macaroons, egg yolk, cream, and Cognac and mix well. Fill each peach half with mixture, mounding it slightly. Arrange in baking dish and bake 40 minutes. Serve cold or hot. Serves 6.

OUTDOOR
DINNER

*Barbecued chicken

*Baked summer
squash casserole

*Herbed garlic bread
(see p. 74)

Sliced tomatoes
vinaigrette

*Strawberries and
peaches in Cointreau

Barbecued chicken

8	ounces tomato ketchup
2	tablespoons chili powder
2	tablespoons prepared mustard
½	cup brown sugar, firmly packed
1	tablespoon freshly ground pepper
¼	cup wine vinegar
2	tablespoons Worcestershire sauce
1	tablespoon soy sauce
2	tablespoons salad oil

Combine all ingredients in a saucepan and whisk together over moderate heat. Cool. Sauce may be refrigerated until needed (it will keep for at least 10 days) or used as soon as it has cooled.

Put 1 or more broiling chickens cut into serving pieces, or the parts you prefer, in a glass or porcelain-lined container and pour enough sauce over to coat each piece well. Cover and marinate in the refrigerator 2–4 hours, turning occasionally.

To cook, preheat oven to 400°.

Remove chicken pieces from marinade and place skin side down in a shallow baking pan. Ideally, the pieces should barely touch.

Bake uncovered for 20 minutes. Turn pieces over, baste with additional sauce, reduce oven heat to 350°, and bake 30 minutes longer. Baste occasionally and check near end of cooking time for doneness—overcooking will produce dry chicken. It is also a good idea to remove the breasts about 10 minutes earlier, as these require less cooking, and keep them warm while rest of chicken is cooking.

Note: This sauce may also be used for charcoal-broiled chicken. Use broilers split in half with backbone removed to lie flat on the grill. If the grill is adjustable, have it in high position. Brush chicken halves with cooking oil.

Place them on the grill skin side up. Brush skin with sauce and let cook 10 minutes. Keep turning and basting until chicken is done (thigh juices should run clear when pricked with a fork, or a small incision at the thigh joint should not reveal any redness around the bone). The sauce is sufficient for three 3-pound chickens.

Baked summer squash casserole

3	pounds yellow summer squash
	Salt
¾	cup bread crumbs (made from fresh bread)
½	cup minced onion
2	eggs, lightly beaten
4	tablespoons butter, melted
½	teaspoon freshly ground pepper
1	tablespoon sugar
	Butter for baking dish

Preheat oven to 375°.

Wash squash, trim ends, cut into 1-inch pieces. Cook in boiling salted water to cover for 10 minutes or until tender.

Drain squash and mash or puree coarsely in a blender or food processor.

Combine bread crumbs with melted butter. Set aside 4 tablespoons of buttered crumbs for the top. Add the squash, onions, eggs, 1 teaspoon salt, pepper to taste, and sugar to remaining crumbs. Butter a 1½-quart baking dish, turn in squash mixture, scatter reserved crumbs on top, and bake for 1 hour, until squash is puffed and crumbs are browned. Serves 6.

Strawberries and peaches in Cointreau

6–8   ripe peaches, peeled
1   quart strawberries, hulled
5   tablespoons sugar, or more to taste
3   tablespoons Cointreau
        Handful chopped mint leaves (optional)

Slice the peaches into a bowl. Halve the strawberries if they are small; quarter them if they are large and add to the bowl. Sugar the fruit, pour the Cointreau over, mix gently, and refrigerate for 2–3 hours before serving.

Garnish with chopped mint leaves if desired. Serves 8.

Steamers

Plan on 1½ to 2 dozen clams per person, depending on size and appetites.

If you have dug the clams yourself, soak them in at least 2 changes of water for 15 minutes each to get rid of excess sand, or soak for 1 hour in water with ¼ cup cornmeal added (the theory is that the clams eat the cornmeal and disgorge sand). Then scrub each well and rinse under running water. If you have a special clam steamer, put them in the top with 2 inches of salted cold water in the bottom. Otherwise put the water in a large kettle and add clams. After water comes to a rolling boil, steam just until the clams open, about 3 minutes. Do not overcook or clams will be rubbery. Discard any that remain closed.

DINNER AFTER A
DAY AT THE
BEACH

*Steamers

*Corn chowder

Mixed green salad

*Frozen orange
cream

Serve with bowls of melted butter, and bowls of the broth. To eat, dip first in broth (this washes off any stubborn sand and seasons the clam), then in the melted butter.

As this menu features soup, save the broth, after straining it through cheesecloth, for use in Bloody Marys, as stock, etc. Ordinarily it is drunk after eating the clams.

Corn chowder

2   medium potatoes, peeled and diced
3   slices bacon, cut in small pieces
1   medium onion, chopped
1½ cups corn kernels (canned or fresh)
1   cup milk
      Salt and pepper to taste

Put potatoes in a pot large enough to hold all the ingredients, add enough boiling water to cover (about 1 cup), a dash of salt, and cook. Meanwhile, sauté bacon until partially rendered of fat. Add onion and sauté until onion is lightly browned and bacon crisp. Add the bacon-onion mixture and about 2 tablespoons of the bacon fat to the potatoes; add the corn and continue cooking until potatoes are just tender. Add milk, salt, and pepper, and heat to just below boiling. Serves 4.

Frozen orange cream

½ cup sugar
1   6-ounce can frozen orange juice concentrate, thawed
1   tablespoon Grand Marnier (or brandy or rum)
    Grated zest (colored skin) of 1 lemon
1   cup heavy cream, whipped
2   egg whites (¼ cup), beaten until stiff but not dry

Dissolve sugar in orange juice and add Grand Marnier and zest.

Lightly fold in whipped cream, then lightly fold in beaten egg whites. Turn into a 1-quart plastic container and place in freezer. Invert every hour or so for 3 or 4 hours until frozen, to prevent settling. This recipe can be doubled or tripled. Serves 6.

Curried fresh corn and green peppers

6–8 tablespoons butter
2   cloves garlic, minced
1   medium onion, chopped
2   tablespoons curry powder
½   teaspoon salt
2   green peppers, seeded and chopped
5–8 ears fresh corn
1   cup heavy cream

Melt butter in heavy skillet and add garlic, onion, curry powder, and salt. Cook over low heat for 5 minutes or until onion is transparent. Add green peppers and sauté for 5 minutes longer.

HOLIDAY BARBECUE

*Curried fresh corn and green peppers

*Striped bass appetizer (see p. 192)

Steak broiled on the grill

*Salad of sliced tomatoes and basil (see p. 29)

*Deep-dish blueberry pie

With a sharp knife, cut the kernels from ears of corn, scraping cobs with back of knife to remove milk. Add corn and corn milk to skillet. Add cream and cook, stirring until mixture just begins to simmer. Cover skillet partially and gently simmer over low heat 15–20 minutes without allowing cream to boil. Serves 6.

Deep-dish blueberry pie

4	cups fresh blueberries (a pint box yields about 3 cups)
4	tablespoons flour
¾–1	cup granulated sugar
¼	cup cornstarch
½	teaspoon nutmeg
	Grated zest (colored skin) of 1 lemon
2	tablespoons butter
½	recipe cream cheese pastry (see p. 233)
1	egg yolk beaten with 1 tablespoon water
	Confectioner's sugar (optional)

Preheat oven to 375°.

Wash and pick over berries. Drain well in a colander and dry on paper towels. Turn into a deep 7-inch-diameter ovenproof dish.

Mix flour, sugar, cornstarch, nutmeg, and lemon zest. Combine with blueberries. Dot with butter.

Roll out pastry to cover, moisten rim of dish and fit on top of pie. Trim edges and crimp. Cut a few slits to allow steam to escape.

Bake in preheated oven 1 hour. Cool on a rack but serve slightly warm. Sprinkle with confectioner's sugar if desired. Serves 6.

Chilled pea and lettuce soup

1	10-ounce box frozen peas, partially thawed, or 1¼ cups shelled fresh
1	medium potato, diced
1	medium onion, chopped
1	head Boston lettuce, quartered
2	cups chicken broth or stock
1	cup heavy cream
	Juice of ½ lemon
	Salt, freshly ground pepper
	Fresh mint (optional)

Put peas, potato, onion, lettuce, and 1 cup of the chicken broth in a saucepan. Bring to the boil. Lower heat, cover, and simmer 10 minutes.

Pour into a blender jar and blend until vegetables are pureed. Return to saucepan, add remaining cup of stock, and simmer 5 minutes. Add cream and lemon juice and season to taste with salt and pepper. Chill. Garnish with mint if desired.

Barbecued marinated leg of lamb

	6-pound leg of lamb, boned and butterflied
1	teaspoon coarsely cracked black pepper
4	cloves garlic, sliced
2	tablespoons vinegar
½	cup red wine
½	cup olive oil
2	bay leaves
½	teaspoon dried thyme
2	teaspoons salt

Spread lamb flat in glass or enamel container. Sprinkle with pepper and garlic. Add remaining ingredients and marinate in refrigerator for 24 hours before cooking.

Remove meat from marinade and cook over very hot coals for 6 minutes each side. Meat should be well browned and crusty. Spread out coals to reduce intensity of heat and continue cooking 6–7 minutes longer *each* side, or a total of 25 minutes. Slice as you would a steak. Serves 8.

Corn on the cob

A word about buying corn. To be avoided at all costs are plastic-wrapped supermarket packets of shucked corn. We address ourselves to corn freshly gathered and eaten as close to picking time as possible. Shortly after corn is picked, the sugar content begins to convert to starch and the flavor begins a subtle change.

Bring salted water to a boil in a large kettle.

Shuck the corn; remove husks, rub silk off with hands or a stiff brush if necessary, break off any undeveloped tips, and put in rapidly boiling water. Bring up to a second boil, cover, and cook 5–8 minutes, depending upon the maturity of the corn. The milk in the kernels will continue to cook even after the corn is removed from the water, so don't overcook—with young tender corn it is only necessary to "set" the milk. Serve with butter and salt.

One easy way to butter corn is to provide small dishes of melted butter and a small inexpensive paintbrush for each person. The corn is then "painted" with the melted butter. Another way to butter corn and not your fingers is to provide each person with a small piece of stale French bread and butter in pats. Butter the piece of bread with the butter pat and run it along the corn one side at a time.

Ratatouille

2   medium eggplants, peeled
4   medium zucchini, unpeeled
    Salt
6   tablespoons olive oil, or more if needed
4   medium onions, thinly sliced
2   small green peppers, seeded and thinly sliced
3   cloves garlic, minced
    Freshly ground black pepper
4–6 tomatoes, peeled, seeded, and juiced
    Bouquet garni composed of a bay leaf, some thyme, and a few parsley sprigs
¼   cup chopped parsley

Prepare the vegetables as indicated in the list of ingredients; slice the eggplants in rounds about ½ inch thick, then cut in large cubes. Cut zucchini in ¼-inch rounds. Toss both vegetables with 2 teaspoons salt in a bowl and let stand for about a half hour. Drain and pat dry with paper towels.

Sauté eggplant and zucchini pieces lightly and quickly in 2 or 3 tablespoons of the oil. Do not have more than a single layer of the vegetables in the frying pan at one time. Add more oil as necessary and remove the sautéed pieces to a warm dish as they are completed.

Put the remaining oil in a heavy enamel-on-cast-iron casserole with a lid and sauté the onions, peppers, and garlic until soft. Season to taste. Add the tomatoes, cover, and cook for 5 minutes. Put ¾ of the mixture in a bowl and spread the remainder over the casserole bottom. Put a layer of ⅓ of the zucchini and eggplant pieces over the tomato-onion mixture and keep layering, ending with the tomatoes. Lightly season each layer with salt and pepper and put the bouquet garni on top. Cover and simmer for ½ hour. Tilt out excess juices into a small pan and cook over high heat until reduced to ¼ cup. Pour this liquid back over the vegetables, raise the heat, and cook uncovered for about 10 minutes. There should be very little liquid left, but the vegetables should still keep their identity.

Remove bouquet garni before serving and sprinkle with fresh chopped parsley. This dish may be served hot, warm, or cold. It may be prepared well in advance of serving and keeps well under refrigeration for several days. Serves 6–8.

Fresh raspberry pie

2	tablespoons minute tapioca
1⅓	cup sugar
4	cups fresh raspberries
½	cup flour
1	teaspoon cinnamon
4	tablespoons butter
1	unbaked 9-inch pastry shell
	Confectioner's sugar
	Whipped cream

Preheat oven to 450°.

Combine tapioca with ⅔ cup sugar and gently mix with raspberries. Allow to sit for 15 minutes. Combine remaining sugar with flour and cinnamon and cut in butter with pastry blender until mixture is crumbly. Spread berry mixture in pie shell. Cover with crumbs. Bake for 10 minutes. Reduce heat to 350° and bake another 30 minutes, or until crust and topping are golden. Allow pie to cool completely. Dust with confectioner's sugar and serve with whipped cream.

Corn pudding

4	eggs
2	cups corn (4–5 ears or 1-pound can creamed)
3	tablespoons flour
1	tablespoon sugar
	Salt, freshly ground pepper
1	cup milk or light cream
1	tablespoon melted butter
	Butter for casserole

Preheat oven to 325°.

Beat eggs until thick; add corn. Combine flour, sugar, and salt and pepper to taste. Slowly stir in milk or cream; then butter. Combine with corn and blend well. Butter a 1½-quart casserole and pour in corn mixture. Bake about 1 hour and 20 minutes, or until a knife inserted in center comes out clean. Serves 4–6.

Broiled striped bass

4	fillets striped bass
	Flour
	Salt, freshly ground pepper
4	tablespoons mayonnaise
4	tablespoons chopped parsley
1½	ounces white wine or dry vermouth
2	tablespoons chopped shallots or green onions
	Lemon wedges

Preheat a broiler oven to 425°.

Lightly oil a baking dish or line the broiler pan with foil, if it will fit in the oven.

Dip fillets in flour, season with salt and pepper, and put skin side down in the baking pan.

Mix the mayonnaise, parsley, wine, and chopped shallots. Add more vermouth if necessary to make a smooth and creamy sauce. Spread mixture over fish and put in the preheated oven for 5 minutes. Then remove from oven, turn heat up to BROIL, and broil until fish is done and the mayonnaise dressing is brown—5–10 minutes, depending on the thickness of the fish. Serve with lemon wedges. Serves 4.

Zucchini and tomatoes

4–5	medium zucchini
1	small onion, sliced
1	clove garlic, minced
2	tablespoons olive oil
2	fresh tomatoes, peeled and chopped
1	teaspoon salt
	Freshly ground pepper
½	bay leaf
1	teaspoon oregano

Wash zucchini and cut into 1-inch slices. Sauté onion in olive oil in a skillet until slightly brown. Stir in garlic and tomatoes and cook 5 minutes longer over medium heat. Add zucchini, salt and pepper to taste, bay leaf, and oregano, and cook gently, covered, 20–25 minutes or until tender.

(If after 15 minutes there appears to be a great deal of liquid in pan, remove cover for the last 5–10 minutes of cooking.) Taste for seasoning, remove bay leaf, and serve immediately. Serves 4.

August blackberry pie

1   recipe cream cheese pastry (see Index)
5   cups ripe blackberries
¼–1 cup sugar, depending on tartness
¼   cup flour
¼   teaspoon lemon juice
3   tablespoons butter

Preheat oven to 400°.

Roll out ⅔ of the pastry and line a 9-inch pie plate with it. *Then* combine blackberries, sugar, flour, and lemon juice. (If you combine the berries and sugar too early, too much juice will form.) Pour filling into pie plate. Dot filling with butter. Roll out a cover with remaining pastry. Put over filling, trim, and crimp edges to seal. Slit the crust in several places and bake about 50 minutes, or until top is well browned. Serve with a slightly softened good French vanilla ice cream. Serves 6.

Note: You may want to place a baking sheet on the rack below the pie. The berry juice often runs.

Weakfish baked with mussels and shrimp

This elegant presentation of a whole fish is really quite simple to prepare, and the mingling of flavorsome ingredients yields a superb natural sauce that will delight dunkers. Striped bass may be substituted for weakfish with equally good results.

1	weakfish, 5 pounds whole, cleaned and gutted, head and tail left on
	Salt and fresh pepper
2–3	branches fresh tarragon or ½ teaspoon dried
	Several parsley branches
6	tablespoons butter
2	medium onions, chopped
¼	pound mushrooms, sliced
¾–1	cup white wine
½	pound mussels, debearded and scrubbed
½	pound uncooked shrimp, shelled and deveined
⅓	cup fresh chopped parsley
3	lemons cut in half

Preheat oven to 375°. Line a broiler pan (or baking dish large enough to hold fish) with heavy baking foil. Set aside.

Wash and dry fish and season with salt and pepper. Stuff with tarragon and parsley branches and set aside.

Melt the butter in the baking pan; add chopped onions, stir to coat them, and bake about 10 minutes or until soft. Add sliced mushrooms and wine, stir, and lay fish on top. Bake 25 minutes.

Put mussels around fish, baste both, and bake 10 minutes longer. Add shrimp, baste everything again, and bake another 10 minutes. At the end of the 45 minutes cooking time, the mussels will be open, the shrimp pink, and the fish baked through. (If using a larger fish, increase the initial baking time accordingly.)

Cover body of fish with chopped parsley and serve right in the baking pan, garnished with lemon halves. Serves 6.

FISH DINNER II

*Weakfish baked with mussels and shrimp

Boiled potatoes

Warmed French bread

Young lettuce salad

*Fresh strawberry pie

Fresh strawberry pie

—adapted from a recipe in the 1924 *LVIS Cookbook*

1	9-inch baked pie shell
1	cup sugar
1	pint fresh ripe strawberries, cleaned and hulled
1	cup heavy cream
2	egg whites
	lemon juice

Preheat oven to 450°. Adjust oven rack to highest position.

Sprinkle bottom of baked pie shell with ¼ cup of the sugar. Fill with the berries. Reserve 2 tablespoons of remaining sugar and sprinkle balance over fruit.

Whip cream until stiff, sweetening to taste if desired. Spread over berries. Beat egg whites with the 2 tablespoons sugar and a dash of lemon juice until stiff and glossy. Carefully spread over cream with a spatula. Put pie in oven just long enough to brown meringue—about 5–7 minutes. Watch carefully and remove from oven the moment meringue is done, so berries will not become heated. Chill thoroughly before serving. Serves 6.

Virtually this entire dinner may be prepared hours to days ahead. The taramasalata may be made and the vegetables for dipping prepared and refrigerated in plastic bags. The stuffed mussels can be done early in the morning and refrigerated on dinner plates covered with a second dinner plate. The moussaka can be done the day before, and sauced and baked just before serving. The salad ingredients, too, can be prepared early and assembled at serving time. The cookies keep for weeks in an airtight container, and, of course, the lemon sherbet may be bought or made when you wish and kept frozen until needed.

MEDITERRANEAN SUMMER BUFFET

Taramasalata with raw vegetables (see p. 184)

*Stuffed mussels

*Moussaka

*Greek salad

Crusty bread

*Thin spice cookies

*Lemon sherbet

Stuffed mussels

3	dozen fresh mussels
	Coarse salt
1½	cups water
½	cup white wine
2	large onions, chopped
¼	cup olive oil
¾	cup raw rice
½	teaspoon cinnamon
½	teaspoon allspice
⅓	cup pignolia nuts
⅓	cup currants
3	tablespoons chopped parsley
	Freshly ground pepper

Clean and debeard mussels and scrub well with a stiff brush under running water. Put in a kettle with the salt, water, and wine. Cover and steam 8–10 minutes or until shells open. Discard any that remain closed. Remove from heat and cool. Strain and reserve liquid.

In a skillet, sauté onions in olive oil until soft; add rice and cook a few minutes longer, stirring constantly.

Add 1½ cups reserved mussel broth and stir in cinnamon, allspice, currants, parsley, and several twists of pepper. Cover, bring to a boil, and cook 15 minutes or until rice is tender and liquid absorbed.

Remove mussels from shells and stir them into the rice. Fill shells with mixture. Chill and serve, garnished with lemon wedges.

Moussaka

5–6	eggplants
	Salt
2	large onions, chopped
½	pound butter
	Olive oil
4	pounds ground lamb or beef or a mixture of both
	Freshly ground pepper
2	cups tomato sauce
	Oregano
	Cinnamon
2–3	cloves garlic, minced
½	cup bread crumbs
1	cup grated Parmesan cheese
8	tablespoons flour
4	cups hot milk
	Nutmeg
6	egg yolks, lightly beaten

Wash eggplants and dry them. Remove stem and blossom ends and cut into ¼-inch slices. Sprinkle with salt, place in a colander, and weight down with a heavy plate while preparing meat.

Melt 8 tablespoons butter and sauté onions until lightly brown. Add the ground meat and brown well. Add salt and pepper to taste, tomato sauce, oregano, cinnamon, and garlic. Cook for an hour, stirring occasionally.

Drain eggplant slices. Arrange on a broiler pan, brush with oil, and broil until lightly brown. Turn slices, brush with oil and broil other side. Remove slices and broil next batch until all are done. Set aside.

Melt the butter in a saucepan, add flour, and cook until mixture froths and is well blended. Do not allow to brown; remove immediately from heat and stir in hot milk. Return to heat and cool until thick and smooth, stirring constantly. Season with salt, freshly ground pepper, and several dashes of nutmeg to taste.

Stir a little of the hot sauce into the beaten egg yolks, then stir egg mixture into sauce, and cook over low heat for a minute or two, stirring constantly. Set aside.

Preheat oven to 375°.

Butter a 10- × 16- × 2-inch baking pan. Combine bread crumbs and ½ cup of the grated cheese and sprinkle on bottom. Make a layer of eggplant slices, overlapping them slightly. Then make a layer of the meat. Continue layers until both eggplant and meat are used, ending with a layer of eggplant. Carefully pour sauce over top, sprinkle with balance of grated cheese, and bake for 1 hour. Cut into squares and serve hot. Serves 14–16.

Greek salad

Boston lettuce
Endive
Romaine
Escarole
Green pepper rings
Cucumber slices
Tomato·wedges
Green onions
Anchovies
Black olives
Feta cheese, crumbled
Lemon vinaigrette
Fresh mint, chopped, (optional)

Use at least 2 or 3 of the greens and any or all of the rest of the ingredients, in quantities compatible with the size of the crowd. Dress with lemon vinaigrette, and sprinkle with the optional mint just before serving.

Thin spice cookies

2¼ cups sifted all-purpose flour
2 teaspoons ground ginger
1 teaspoon ground cinnamon
1 teaspoon ground cardamom
½ teaspoon ground cloves
1 teaspoon salt
12 tablespoons butter or margarine
½ cup sugar
½ cup dark corn syrup
1 tablespoon brandy
1 tablespoon lemon juice
1 tablespoon grated lemon zest (colored skin)

Sift flour, spices, and salt onto waxed paper.

Cream butter or margarine and sugar in a large bowl and beat until fluffy; beat in corn syrup, brandy, lemon juice, and zest. Stir in flour mixture, blending well to make a soft dough. Chill well several hours or overnight.

Divide dough in 4 pieces. Roll each out very thinly between a sheet of foil and a sheet of waxed paper, to a rectangle about 12 by 16 inches. Peel waxed paper from top and place foil with dough on large cookie sheet. Score into squares or rectangles in a desired size with tip of a very sharp knife.

Bake in a 350° oven 10 minutes or until pale golden brown. Cookies will appear soft, but will harden. Place foil on wire rack and allow cookies to cool. Carefully remove cookies from foil and break apart along scored lines. It is essential to store these cookies in an airtight container. Makes about 60 cookies.

Lemon Sherbet

3   teaspoons gelatin
½   cup cold water
4½   cups warm water
1½   cups sugar
2   teaspoons grated lemon zest (colored skin)
1½   cups fresh lemon juice
4   egg whites, stiffly beaten

Soak the gelatin in the cold water. Combine the warm water and sugar, bring to a boil and boil for 10 minutes. Off heat, dissolve the gelatin mixture in the hot syrup. Allow to cool, chill in refrigerator, then stir in grated lemon zest and lemon juice. Fold in the stiffly beaten egg whites, put in freezer trays, cover with foil, and freeze. Serves 10.

Paella

SIMPLE BUFFET DINNER

With Drinks:

Crudités with guacamole (see p. 183)

*Paella

Garlic bread (see p. 74)

Salad of Boston and Ruby lettuce and curly endive

*Coeur à la Crème

This dish has almost all the virtues necessary for a good party dish: It can be stretched infinitely by the addition of rice; it can be made in large quantities, and it does not suffer from standing. There are many versions of paella, with additions and variations made according to the locally available items. Strictly speaking, in Valencia where it originated, paella contains chicken, pork—in the form of sausages or fat pork—olive oil, garlic, tomatoes, and seafood or shellfish. Fresh peas or chopped green or red peppers are sometimes added.

Paella may be cooked in a deep good-size frying pan, but for best results it should be made in a special pan also called a paella. If you are going to cook paella from time to time, it is worth investing in and is available in most good cookware shops.

	Olive oil
2	small chickens, cut in 8 pieces each, or 8 legs and 8 thighs
	Flour
1	to 1½ pounds squid, cleaned (optional)
1	chorizo sausage or 6 Italian sausages (hot or sweet)
12–18	mussels
1	cup chopped onion
3	cloves garlic, chopped
1	medium green pepper, cut in strips
2	cups raw rice (not instant)
12–16	large shrimp, peeled and deveined
3	large fresh tomatoes, peeled, seeded, and chopped, or 1½ cups canned tomatoes, drained and chopped
	Powdered saffron
4	cups liquid: combination of heated chicken broth and mussel broth
	Salt, freshly ground pepper
	Lemon wedges
	Pimiento strips

Heat 2–3 tablespoons olive oil in the paella pan: dredge chicken pieces with flour, and gently sauté them until golden brown all over. Set aside while preparing the other ingredients.

If you have been able to obtain squid, cut in rings, sauté in olive oil, and set aside.

If using Italian sausages, cover with cold water in a shallow skillet and bring to a boil. Cook over high heat, uncovered, until water boils away. Prick occasionally to release fat, then turn heat down and fry until brown. Drain and cut into 2-inch pieces. If using chorizo, it is not necessary to cook it. Cut into 2-inch pieces.

Scrub mussels and steam them open. Remove them from shells and keep as many of the best shell halves as you have mussels. Strain the broth; set aside.

Add more olive oil to pan if necessary and sauté onion and garlic until transparent. Add pepper strips and cook 10 minutes longer. Add rice and cook slowly in the oil for about 5 minutes, stirring constantly until most of the grains have become opaquely white. Do not let them scorch or brown.

Stir in shrimp and chopped tomatoes. Dissolve saffron in a little chicken broth and stir into rest of liquid. Add to pan. Season very well with salt and pepper, bring to a boil, lower heat, and simmer gently for 5 minutes. Stir in squid and sausage pieces and arrange chicken pieces around perimeter of pan. Continue cooking for about 15 minutes more or until the rice is tender but the grains are separate (if mixture looks too dry before rice is cooked, lower heat; if it still looks too moist, increase heat).

Arrange mussels and pimiento strips on top of rice. Turn off heat and cover pan with a clean tea towel to absorb excess moisture. Garnish with lemon wedges and serve. Serves 8–10.

Note: Other ingredients you may add to paella are: small pieces of fried pork, pieces of cooked lobster, tiny clams, peas, or mushrooms. You can also use more rice, always keeping the 2-cups-liquid-to-1-cup-rice proportion.

Coeur à la Crème

4	ounces cream cheese
	Salt
8	ounces creamed cottage cheese
½	vanilla bean
1	cup heavy cream
½	cup sugar
	Strawberries
	Raspberry sauce (see p. 14)

Line a 3-cup heart mold or 6 small porcelain molds with a double layer of cheesecloth soaked in cold water and wrung out. Be sure cloth extends well over sides of mold(s). Chill.

Whip cream cheese with a wooden spatula until fluffy; slowly add ¼ cup sugar and a pinch of salt. Whip in cottage cheese. Slit vanilla bean lengthwise and scrape seeds into cheese mixture. Mix well.

Beat cream in a chilled metal bowl until firm, slowly adding remaining ¼ cup sugar. Lightly fold sweetened cream into cheese mixture and combine well.

Spoon mixture into cloth-lined mold(s), bringing cheesecloth over top. Set mold(s) in a pan and let drain overnight in refrigerator.

Unmold, peel cloth off, surround with strawberries and accompany with raspberry sauce. Serves 6. Make two for a buffet.

Note: If a number of small hearts is required, the same molds can be used for double duty by letting a second batch of the cheese mixture drain tied in cheesecloth hanging over the inside of a bowl overnight while the first batch is being done. Then do a second round of molds with the drained cheese, chilling for at least 6 hours.

Paprikash chicken

This is one of those dishes that actually benefits from being made ahead, since the flavors seem to ripen and mature. The tasty sauce makes serving with noodles (or rice, if you prefer) a must.

2	large onions, chopped
1	clove garlic, minced
6	tablespoons cooking fat or oil
½	green pepper, shredded
	Hungarian semisweet paprika
3	3½-pound young chickens, cut up
	Salt
1	small ripe tomato, peeled, seeded, chopped
1¼	cups chicken stock
1	cup sour cream, scalded
	Freshly ground pepper

Sauté onions and garlic in fat or oil in either a heavy large skillet with a cover or a Dutch oven. Add pepper and 2 tablespoons paprika and mix well. Sprinkle chickens lightly with salt, add to the skillet, and mix in tomato. Pour in 1 cup chicken stock, mix, and bring to a boil, then cover, lower heat, and simmer slowly, turning chicken from time to time, until tender (about 25 minutes). Adjust seasoning with salt and pepper to taste.

Transfer chicken to warm platter. Add remaining stock and bring to a boil, scraping bits from bottom and sides. Add sour cream, more paprika if desired, and stir till smooth. Pour over chicken and serve with buttered noodles. Serves 6–8.

HUNGARIAN DINNER

*Paprikash chicken

Buttered noodles

*Sweet-and-sour purple cabbage

*Applesauce

*Cucumber salad

*Cheesecake

Sweet-and-sour purple cabbage

1   red cabbage (4 to 5 pounds)
3   tablespoons butter
1   cup finely chopped onions
3   tablespoons cider vinegar
3   tablespoons brown sugar or more to taste
1   teaspoon salt
    Freshly ground black pepper

Remove any tough bruised outer leaves. Cut cabbage in quarters, remove core, and shred very thinly, using either a large heavy knife or the slicing disc of a food processor. Soak cabbage in cold water for a few minutes.

Heat butter in a large heavy pot and sauté onions until soft, about 5 minutes. Drain cabbage and add. Mix vinegar, sugar, salt, and a generous amount of pepper and pour over cabbage. Cover pot and cook slowly over low heat until cabbage is tender (25–40 minutes, depending upon age of cabbage). Taste and correct sweet-sour balance if needed.

Drain and serve in a heated serving dish. Serves 6–8.

Applesauce

5–6   pounds early McIntosh or Cortland apples
½   cup lemon juice
      Sugar

Wash apples, remove stems and blossom ends. Cut in quarters. Put lemon juice in a large heavy pot (do not use aluminum) and add all the apples. Cook covered over a very low flame, stirring occasionally, until the apples are reduced to mush. This will take about 1 hour. No other liquid is necessary, but if you do not trust your low flame, cook on an asbestos mat to prevent scorching.

Put everything through a foodmill (skins, seeds, core, etc. will be held back). Sweeten the puree to taste and return briefly to a low fire just long enough to melt the sugar. Serve as a side dish. Makes 3–4 quarts.

Cucumber salad

3	large cucumbers
2	tablespoons salt
⅓	cup water
5	tablespoons vinegar
1	tablespoon sugar
½	teaspoon freshly ground white pepper
2	tablespoons minced dill or parsley

Peel cucumbers, and slice them paper-thin. Sprinkle with the salt, cover, weight down, and let stand refrigerated for several hours or overnight. Drain well, pressing on the cucumbers to extract all the moisture.

Combine water, vinegar, sugar, and pepper. Pour over cucumbers and marinate in refrigerator 1–2 hours. Sprinkle with dill or parsley before serving. Serves 6–8.

Cheesecake

Butter for pan
20 pieces zwieback, crushed with 2 tablespoons sugar and 2 tablespoons melted butter
6 eggs, separated
1½ cups sugar
18 ounces cream cheese
2 tablespoons flour
1 teaspoon lemon extract
⅛ teaspoon salt
1½ cup sour cream
⅓ cup milk

Preheat oven to 350°.

Butter a 9-inch springform pan and line with buttered and sugared crumbs.

Beat egg yolks well. Blend cream cheese with sugar and egg yolks, beating until it is thoroughly creamed. Add 2 tablespoons sugar, flour, and lemon extract and mix well.

Add 1 cup sour cream, mix remaining ½ cup sour cream with milk, and blend into cheese mixture.

Beat egg whites until stiff but not dry. Fold in. Pour into the prepared mold and bake at 350° for 1 hour.

Turn off oven heat, set oven door ajar, and leave cake in open oven for an additional hour. Unmold and serve. Serves 12.

Chicken with tomato shallot sauce

2	2½-pound chickens, cut into serving pieces
	Salt, freshly ground pepper
6	tablespoons butter
1	cup sliced fresh mushrooms
1½	cups tomatoes, peeled, seeded, and chopped
¼	cup finely chopped shallots
½	cup dry white wine
1	teaspoon chopped fresh thyme or ½ teaspoon dried
1	tablespoon chopped fresh tarragon
1½	cups heavy cream

Sprinkle the chicken with salt and pepper.

Heat 4 tablespoons butter in a large heavy skillet and brown the chicken on all sides. Cover and cook slowly about 30 minutes or until tender.

In a separate skillet, cook the mushrooms in the remaining butter until wilted. Set aside.

Remove the chicken and keep it warm. Add the shallots to the skillet and cook briefly, stirring. Add the tomatoes, wine, mushrooms, thyme, and tarragon. Cook 10 to 15 minutes, then add the cream. Season to taste with salt and pepper. Return the chicken to the skillet and heat gently until chicken and sauce are hot. Do not let sauce boil. Serves 4–6.

ELEGANT CHICKEN DINNER

*Bacon-broiled clams
(see p. 191)

*Chicken with tomato
shallot sauce

Rice

Salad of Boston
lettuce and watercress

*Chocolate roll

Chocolate roll

No flour is used in this delicate cake.

ROLL:

	Butter for pan
3	eggs at room temperature
5	tablespoons superfine sugar
3	tablespoons unsweetened cocoa
1	teaspoon vanilla
½	teaspoon almond extract
½	teaspoon cinnamon

FILLING:

1½	cups heavy cream
2	tablespoons unsweetened cocoa
¼	cup granulated sugar
½	teaspoon vanilla extract

Preheat oven to 350°.

Butter a 10- × 14-inch jelly roll pan and line carefully with waxed paper, cut one inch longer than pan (this gives a ''handle'' for easier removal after baking).

Make roll: Separate eggs; beat yolks and sugar together until they are creamy yellow and form a ribbon. Sift cocoa through a strainer and stir in. Stir in vanilla, almond extract, and cinnamon.

Beat egg whites until they form definite peaks; then fold the cocoa mixture into the whites very gently with a rubber spatula.

Pour into prepared pan and bake 15–18 minutes or until cake pulls away slightly from sides of pan. Cool pan on a rack for 5 minutes, then with one quick movement turn cake out onto a slightly dampened tea towel. Carefully peel off waxed paper.

Make the filling: Combine cream, sugar, cocoa, and vanilla in a bowl. Chill in refrigerator 1–2 hours; then beat mixture until stiff but not hard. Spread half the mixture on the cooled cake, and roll up gently. Put on serving dish and cover top with remaining whipped cream mixture. Serves 6.

Potage Mongole

1   can condensed tomato soup (10¾ ounces)
1   can condensed green pea soup (10¾ ounces)
1¼ cups hot milk
½   cup chicken stock or broth
1   teaspoon Worcestershire sauce
1   teaspoon curry powder or to taste
    Sherry

Mix the 2 soups together in a saucepan and gradually stir in the hot milk over low heat. Stir until smooth and add the stock or broth, Worcestershire, and curry. Cook at just below the simmer 8–10 minutes. Do not boil. Taste for seasoning. Serve in heated soup cups with a splash of sherry added to each at the last minute. Serves 6.

Crisp pita bread

Buy packaged Middle Eastern flat bread (pita bread). Cut rounds into 4 parts with a kitchen scissors. Carefully spread open and butter insides top and bottom with softened butter. Place triangles on a cookie sheet and bake at 300° for 30 minutes or until light brown and crisp.

These can be made ahead, frozen, and reheated when needed. Good with all sorts of soups and dips.

DINNER FOR THE FIRST COLD DAY

*Potage Mongole

*Crisp pita bread

*Loin of pork stuffed with prunes

*Puree of potatoes and celery root

Watercress salad

*Crème brulée

Loin of pork stuffed with prunes

1	center-cut loin of pork, boned but not rolled, weighing 3½–4 pounds
2	tablespoons salt
	Freshly ground black pepper
1½	teaspoons thyme
½	teaspoon crumbled bay leaf
	Allspice
1	clove garlic, put through a press
2	medium onions, chopped
5	tablespoons butter
6–8	ounces pitted prunes, coarsely chopped
½	teaspoon thyme
¼	cup chopped parsley
2	tablespoons oil
1	cup chicken broth
	Water
½–1	cup heavy cream
8–12	whole prunes plumped in tea or Madeira

Mix the salt, a liberal amount of pepper, 1 teaspoon of the thyme, bay leaf, allspice, and garlic. Rub and pat all over the pork and let marinate 12–14 hours. Scrape this dry marinade off the pork before proceeding.

Sauté onions in 3 tablespoons butter until soft; add prunes, remaining ½ teaspoon thyme, and parsley, and cook a few minutes more.

Lay the pork loin flat with the boned or ''wrong'' side up, and spoon stuffing over. Roll and tie with thin white string. Preheat oven to 350°. Melt the butter in the oil in a heavy casserole or Dutch oven just big enough to hold the pork. Brown meat slowly on all sides (some stuffing may ooze out; this is perfectly all right). It will take about 15–20 minutes.

Bring to a simmer on top of stove, add chicken broth and enough water to half cover the meat, cover, put in oven, and simmer 1½ hours.

Remove meat and keep warm. Stir sauce well, then put the sauce through a sieve. Skim off any fat. Correct the seasoning. Stir in the cream over moderate heat, but do not boil. Slice the pork and arrange on a warm platter, and pour the sauce over. Garnish with whole prunes. Serves 8.

Puree of potatoes and celery root

2⅓ pounds celery knob (also called celery root, celeriac, and *celeri-rave*)
2 cups warm mashed potatoes
Chopped parsley
Butter
Salt, freshly ground white pepper
1½ cups chicken stock or water

Peel celery root and cut into ½-inch slices. Put in saucepan with 2 tablespoons butter and enough stock or water to barely cover. Season lightly with salt and pepper, bring to a boil, cover, and boil slowly 20–30 minutes or until tender. If any liquid remains, uncover pot and cook over high heat until it evaporates.

Puree celery root in a food processor and mix well into mashed potatoes. Warm the puree briefly, stir in an additional lump of butter, correct seasoning, and sprinkle with parsley. Serves 8.

Crème brulée

4   cups heavy cream
4   tablespoons sugar
8   egg yolks
    Salt
2   teaspoons vanilla extract
    Light brown sugar

Preheat oven to 350°.

Scald the cream; add sugar and stir until dissolved. Beat egg yolks well with a pinch of salt.

Add a few drops of the scalded cream to the yolks to warm them, then the rest in a slow steady stream. Stir in vanilla.

Pour into a shallow baking dish; depth of the custard should be about 4 inches. (A porcelain gratin dish or a Pyrex baking dish is ideal.) Put this dish carefully into a larger pan filled with enough hot water to come halfway up side of baking dish. Bake for 40 minutes or until a knife inserted in center comes out clean.

Cool on a rack, then chill in refrigerator until shortly before serving time. Sift brown sugar evenly over top to a depth of ¼ inch. Put briefly under broiler flame and turn dish as required (watching very carefully, as it can burn easily) until sugar is melted and just carmelized.

Chill again briefly and serve. A light tap of the spoon breaks the glaze. Serves 6 to 8.

Watercress soup

4	medium potatoes, peeled
	Chicken stock (optional)
1	small onion, peeled and halved
1	bunch watercress, stems removed
	Salt, freshly ground pepper to taste
	Butter
½–1	cup cream

Parboil potatoes. Reserving water, cube potatoes and return to pot with 3 cups of liquid (the potato water alone or in combination with chicken broth). Add onion, put watercress on top, and simmer covered 8–10 minutes.

Puree in blender or food processor until watercress is reduced to tiny green flecks. (Depending on blender capacity, it may have to be done in 2 batches.)

Add salt and pepper to taste, stir in a good lump of butter, and add cream according to richness desired.

Heat, but do not boil. If soup appears too thick, thin with some boiling water or leftover potato water. Serves 4–6.

Note: This soup may be made well in advance of serving time.

DUCK DINNER

*Watercress soup

*Roast duckling à l'orange

*Mock wild rice with mushrooms

Green salad

*Brandied peaches with crème anglaise

Roast duckling à l'orange

The late Henri Soulé, who ran the Hedges restaurant in East Hampton, gave this recipe to the LVIS.

2	ducks (4–5 pounds each)
	Salt, freshly ground pepper
2	oranges
1	cup consommé or beef stock
2	tablespoons sugar
1	teaspoon arrowroot
½	cup Cointreau or curaçao

Preheat oven to 425°.

Clean ducks and trim off all loose fat. Truss, then prick fatty areas with a fork. Salt and pepper skin.

Put ducks in a large roasting pan and pour ½ cup water over. Roast 1 hour.

While duck is roasting, remove the zest (colored skin) from the oranges, using a potato peeler. Cut skin in fine julienne. Put peel in saucepan and cover with cold water. Bring to a boil and simmer 5 minutes. Drain and run cold water over. Set aside. Then strip off white pith and discard. Section orange for garnish.

Remove ducks from pan and pour off fat. Return ducks to pan, add gizzards and necks, and roast 1 hour more, or until well cooked and brown. Keep ducks warm while you make the sauce; skim fat from pan juices, add consommé or stock, put pan on top of stove, bring to a boil and add arrowroot diluted in a little water. Let boil a few minutes, scraping up brown bits from bottom and sides. Correct seasoning with salt if necessary, and strain. Set aside.

Put sugar in a small saucepan and carmelize it lightly over high heat. Moisten with a few spoonfuls of the duck sauce and stir until smooth. Add remaining sauce and julienne of orange.

When ready to serve, add orange liqueur. Garnish duck with orange slices and pour sauce over. Serves 4–6.

Mock wild rice with mushrooms

1   large onion, finely chopped
2   tablespoons cooking oil
2   tablespoons butter
1   pound fresh mushrooms, finely chopped
2   tablespoons soy sauce
2   cups uncooked Carolina rice, washed
4   cups chicken broth, heated
    Chopped parsley

Sauté onion in butter and oil until transparent. Add mushrooms and cook about 5 minutes, stirring until mushrooms give up their water and it evaporates. Stir in soy sauce and cook for a few minutes longer to blend.

Add a little more butter if pan is very dry, then add rice and cook 3–4 minutes, until rice is coated and brown. Add chicken broth, stir, bring to a boil, cover and lower heat. Cook until rice is tender and all liquid absorbed, about 20 minutes. Serve garnished with chopped parsley. Serves 4 to 6.

Brandied peaches with crème anglaise

Use a very good commercial brand of brandied peaches, or homemade. Put peaches and their juice in a ovenproof dish, cover with foil, and warm in a slow oven.

Serve with crème anglaise (see p. 242).

ONE-DISH DINNER

*Veal with peppers and potatoes

Arugula salad

Sesame bread sticks with butter

*Pear and ricotta cheese pie

Veal with peppers and potatoes

4	loin veal chops
6	tablespoons olive oil
1	medium onion, sliced
3	large green peppers, washed, seeded, and cut into thin strips
2	cloves garlic
4	medium potatoes, sliced
	Salt, freshly ground pepper
	Chopped parsley

Brown veal chops in 3 tablespoons of oil in a heavy skillet. Set aside and keep warm. Add remaining oil and sauté onion, peppers, garlic, and potatoes. When peppers and potatoes are lightly browned and soft, add veal, season with salt and pepper to taste, and cover. Cook slowly for about 30 minutes or until veal is well done. Serve sprinkled with chopped parsley. Serves 4.

Pear and ricotta cheese pie

8	fresh ripe pears
1½	cups water
1	cup sugar
	Grated zest (colored skin) and juice of ½ lemon
¼	cup black raisins
¼	cup golden raisins
	Brandy
	Butter
1	box zwieback biscuits
8	ounces ricotta cheese
¼	cup granulated sugar
3	egg yolks, well beaten
½	teaspoon almond extract
1	tablespoon cornstarch

Peel and core the pears. Combine the water, sugar, and lemon juice, bring to a boil, and simmer 5 minutes. Add the pears, cover, and poach for about 12 minutes or until the fruit can be easily pierced with the tip of a sharp knife. Let cool in the syrup, remove, and drain, reserving syrup.

While pears are cooking, plump raisins by soaking in brandy. Drain them and dry.

Make a crust by mixing zwieback crumbs and softened butter according to the zwieback package instructions. Butter a 9-inch springform cake mold or a 9-inch Pyrex pie plate and line with the crust.

Slice 3 pears and arrange on bottom of pan. Whip ricotta cheese with sugar, then stir in egg yolks and almond extract. Fold in raisins and grated lemon zest. Dice 2 pears and fold in. Fill lined cake mold with this mixture to within ¼ inch from the top. Bake in a 375° oven for 25 minutes. Cool on a rack, then chill in refrigerator.

Bring the poaching liquid to the boil and simmer until reduced by half, or until it is about 1 cup. Mix the cornstarch with a little cold water to dissolve it. Add to syrup and cook for a few minutes to thicken. Cool.

Slice the remaining pears into ¾-inch slices and arrange in a decorative layer over the top of the cake, and glaze with the syrup. Chill until set. Serves 6.

Baked potatoes with Boursin

When baked potatoes are removed from the oven, split them open, salt and pepper them, and top each with a large dollop of Boursin cheese (the kind flavored with garlic and herbs). It is a nice variation on the sour-cream-with-chives dressing.

Have more Boursin available on the table.

Scalloped carrots and celery with caraway seeds

4	tablespoons butter
¼	cup chopped onions
3	cups celery, thinly sliced on the diagonal
3	cups carrots, thinly sliced on the diagonal
¼	cup chicken broth or stock
½	teaspoon salt
	Freshly ground pepper to taste
1	teaspoon caraway seeds

Melt butter and sauté onions; do not let them brown. Add celery, carrots, salt, pepper, and broth. Cover, bring to a boil, lower heat, and simmer 10–15 minutes or until vegetables are tender but still slightly crisp. Uncover, raise heat slightly, and cook 2–3 minutes to evaporate any excess liquid.

Toss with caraway just before serving. Serves 6–8.

DINNER WITH THE CHILDREN

Roast beef
(see p. 99)

*Baked potatoes
with Boursin

*Scalloped carrots
and celery with
caraway seeds

Green salad

Chocolate ice cream
with ginger cookies
(see p. 227)

EAST

Special Occasions

HAMPTON

*S*ometime in late June, back in the 1890s, the LVIS ladies would spread trestle tables with white damask cloths and raise funds for their good works with a Strawberry Festival. There would be a choice of hot short-cake smothered in cold strawberries and dripping with cream; homemade strawberry ice cream with cake, fresh strawberries and cream, layer cake, and oceans of coffee. That was supper, with second and third helpings served cheerfully by bustling housewives in their best white aprons.

Our modern version caters to the current come-for-dessert-and-coffee custom.

Old-fashioned strawberry shortcake

2	cups flour
1	tablespoon baking powder
¼	teaspoon salt
10	tablespoons butter at room temperature
½	cup milk, approximately
2	pints very ripe strawberries, washed, hulled, and dried
	Sugar
1	cup heavy cream, whipped

Preheat oven to 400°.

Sift together the flour, baking powder and salt. Cut in one stick of the butter with a pastry blender. Then, mixing with a fork, add just enough milk to make a soft dough. Stir carefully while blending, then vigorously for a minute, until dough leaves sides of bowl.

Turn dough onto a lightly floured board and *knead gently with a light hand* for half a minute. Divide in half, and with lightly floured hands pat each portion onto the bottom of an inverted 8-inch cake pan. Prick the surface in several places with a fork. Bake in preheated oven for 15 minutes or until golden.

Meanwhile, crush berries and sweeten to taste.

When cakes are done, spread one with the remaining butter, while still hot. Put the layer on a serving plate, spread with half the strawberries, top with second layer, then the remaining strawberries. Cut cake into six equal wedges and serve warm with plain or whipped cream. Serves 6.

Grand Marnier sauce

This sauce is very easy to make but requires improvising a special double boiler; a regular one will not do for this recipe.

5   egg yolks
½   cup plus 2 tablespoons sugar
¼   cup Grand Marnier
1   cup heavy cream

Find a saucepan in which you can snugly sit a 2-quart mixing bowl so that the bottom of the bowl clears the bottom of the pot by about 3 inches. Put 2 inches of water in the pot and bring to a boil.

Put the yolks and ½ cup sugar in bowl; beat for 2 minutes with a hand beater; be sure to scrape around insides of bowl.

Put bowl on the pot of boiling water (it must not touch water). Continue beating for 10 minutes or until mixture is pale yellow and thick. Remove bowl from pot and stir in half the Grand Marnier. Cook, then chill well.

Beat cream with 2 tablespoons sugar until almost stiff. Fold cream into chilled sauce, stir in balance of Grand Marnier. Serves 10.

LVIS Fair Cake

Butter and flour for pan
⅔ cup butter
1½ cups sugar
3 eggs
2½ cups sifted cake flour
2¼ cups sifted all-purpose flour
2½ teaspoons baking powder
½ teaspoon salt
1 cup milk
1 teaspoon vanilla

Butter and flour two 9-inch-diameter layer cake pans. Preheat oven to 350°.

Cream butter until light; add sugar and continue creaming until light and fluffy.

Add the eggs one at a time, beating well after each.

Sift together the two flours, baking powder, and salt. Add alternately to butter mixture with the milk, blending well after each addition. Stir in vanilla. Pour batter into prepared pans. Bake for about 25 minutes or until a tester comes clean.

FLUFFY FROSTING:
1½ cups sugar
½ cup water
1 tablespoon light corn syrup
2 egg whites, stiffly beaten
1 teaspoon vanilla

Combine sugar, water, and corn syrup. Bring to a boil and cook to 230° on a candy thermometer or until mixture spins a thread.

Pour hot syrup very gradually over the stiffly beaten whites, stirring and blending constantly. Stir in vanilla.

When of spreading consistency, spread over tops and sides of cake.

162   SPECIAL OCCASIONS

CHOCOLATE DRIZZLE:

2   ounces unsweetened chocolate
⅓   cup sugar
¼   cup water
1   teaspoon butter

Melt the chocolate over hot water.

Combine sugar and water in a small saucepan. Bring to a boil and cook 30 seconds, stirring constantly. Swirl in butter and stir until blended.

Remove from heat and let cool, stirring from time to time until mixture is of spreading consistency. Drizzle over frosted cake so that chocolate runs down sides at intervals in a drip effect.

Pound cake

Butter and flour for cake pan
½   pound unsalted butter
1–⅔   cups sugar
5   eggs
2   cups flour, sifted 5 times
1   tablespoon rose water
1   teaspoon vanilla

Preheat oven to 325°. Butter and flour a 9- or 10-inch tube cake pan.

Cream butter until fluffy. Add sugar and continue creaming until all traces of sugar grains have disappeared.

Add the eggs, 1 at a time, beating well after each addition is completely absorbed.

Add flour in small quantities, beating very hard after each addition. Add rose water and vanilla and mix well.

Spoon carefully into prepared pan. Bake 50 to 60 minutes. Cool slightly in the pan, then turn out onto a rack and cool completely before slicing.

A TEA PARTY

*Pound cake

*Viennese chocolate cherry torte

*Lemon-nut tea bread

*Apricot squares

*Swedish cookies

Cucumber and watercress sandwiches

Viennese chocolate cherry torte

Butter and flour for pan
½ cup plus 2 tablespoons butter
½ cup (scant) sugar
3 ounces semisweet chocolate, melted
3 eggs at room temperature, separated
4 tablespoons flour
6 tablespoons finely ground walnuts
1 cup canned tart red cherries, well drained

GLAZE:
6 ounces semisweet chocolate
¼ cup strong coffee

Preheat oven to 350°. Butter and flour a 9-inch springform pan.

Cream butter well; add sugar and continue creaming until light and fluffy. Beat in melted chocolate, then egg yolks. Blend well.

Beat egg whites until stiff but not dry. Combine flour and nuts and fold into chocolate mixture alternately with the egg whites.

Spoon mixture into prepared pan. Drop cherries evenly over top of batter. Bake for 55 minutes. Cool pan thoroughly on a rack before removing cake to a decorative plate.

Make the glaze by melting the 6 ounces of chocolate in the coffee. Spread over top and sides of cake. Serves 8–10.

Lemon-nut tea bread

This old Shaker recipe makes a delightful cake that freezes extremely well.

BREAD:

1½	cups flour
1	teaspoon baking powder
	Butter for pan
2	eggs, beaten
¼	pound butter, melted
1	cup sugar
	Salt
½	cup chopped walnuts
	Grated zest (colored skin) of 1 lemon

GLAZE:

	Juice of 1 large lemon
⅓	cup sugar

Preheat oven to 350°. Butter an 8½- × 4½- × 2½-inch loaf pan.

Sift together flour and baking powder. Add eggs, butter, sugar, a dash of salt, walnuts, and lemon zest, and beat together well. Pour into prepared loaf pan and bake for 50 minutes or until a tester comes out clean.

While bread is still hot, mix together lemon juice and sugar for the glaze and pour over bread. Then cool thoroughly before removing from pan.

Apricot squares

This is an attractive and satisfying dessert pastry that freezes exceptionally well.

FILLING:

1	cup tightly packed dried apricots, finely cut up (about one 11-ounce pack)
1	cup butterscotch morsels (one 6-ounce pack)
	Grated zest (colored skin) of 1 lemon
¼	cup lemon juice
¼	cup water

Combine all the ingredients to make a sauce. Cook over medium heat, stirring constantly until blended and thickened, about 10 minutes.

PASTRY:

¼	pound butter
1	cup all-purpose flour
½	cup sugar
1	egg yolk
	Grated zest of 1 lemon
½	teaspoon vanilla
	Butter and flour for baking dish
1	egg yolk, beaten with 1 tablespoon water

Blend butter and flour until it has the texture of oatmeal. Blend in sugar, egg yolk, lemon zest, and vanilla. Form into a ball.

Preheat oven to 350°. Butter and flour a 7- × 11-inch shallow baking dish.

Put about half the pastry in the bottom of baking dish, patting it down to fit. Bake until very pale gold, about 10 minutes. Cool.

Spread apricot filling over pastry. Roll out remaining dough thinly, cut strips, and top the apricot filling with a lattice pattern.

Brush top with egg yolk mixture to give it a pretty color, and bake until lightly brown, about 15 minutes. Watch it carefully at this stage as it can burn easily.

Cool and cut into squares. Makes about 35 squares.

Note: If these pastries are frozen, they should be left out at room temperature, tightly wrapped, to defrost.

Swedish cookies

¼	pound butter
¼	cup light brown sugar, firmly packed
1	egg, separated
1	cup flour
	Salt
½	teaspoon vanilla
¾	cup finely chopped walnuts (approximately 3½ ounces nut halves)
	Red currant jelly

Cream butter and sugar. Add egg yolk and flour with a pinch of salt. Add vanilla and mix well. Chill for 2 hours.

Shape the dough into small balls (1 inch in diameter). Coat with egg white and roll in the chopped walnuts. Put on baking sheet. Bake in a 300° oven for 15 minutes. Press a small hole in the center of each cookie and fill with red currant jelly.

Bake another 25 minutes.

Makes approximately 22 cookies. These cookies freeze well.

Spiced cider

2	teaspoons ground nutmeg
4	tablespoons allspice
4	cloves
4	cinnamon sticks
	Juice of 4 oranges
	Juice of 2 lemons
1	cup granulated sugar
2	quarts sweet apple cider
4	baked apples (optional)

Combine the spices, fruit juice, sugar, and cider. Bring to a boil and stir until sugar is dissolved.

Slice the optional baked apples and place in a punch bowl; strain the boiling hot cider over them and serve.

Some strong tea may be added, and/or rum. Serves 10–12.

Chestnut oyster stuffing

¼	pound butter
1	can (15½-ounce) chestnut puree
	Salt, freshly ground pepper
1	cup chopped celery
4	tablespoons chopped parsley
4	tablespoons grated onion
3	tablespoons chopped chives
6	cups coarse bread crumbs
1	egg
12	oysters

Melt 2 tablespoons of butter and stir into chestnut puree; season to taste with salt and pepper.

Sauté celery in 4 tablespoons of butter until soft. Add parsley, onions, and chives, and toss mixture with bread crumbs and chestnut puree in a large bowl. Add egg and mix well.

Drain oysters, chop coarsely, and poach for 2 minutes in 2 tablespoons of butter. Toss lightly with stuffing. Allow to sit awhile. Sufficient to stuff a 10–14 pound bird.

Braised brussels sprouts

1	quart brussels sprouts
4	tablespoons butter
½	cup chicken broth
	Salt and freshly ground pepper

Remove any dark leaves and trim stems of sprouts. Put them in a large pot of rapidly boiling salted water. Bring again to the boil, lower heat, and boil slowly, uncovered, 7–8 minutes. Drain.

Melt butter in a skillet, add sprouts and cook over rather high heat for several minutes. Add broth, bring to a simmer, cover, and cook over low heat about 10–12 minutes, or until sprouts are tender but not mushy and most of broth is absorbed. Should too much liquid remain, cook uncovered 3–4 minutes. Season to taste. Serves 4.

Escalloped sweet potatoes

5 medium sweet potatoes or yams
2 tart apples, skins on
   Butter for casserole
¾ teaspoon salt
½ cup brown sugar
3 tablespoons butter

Preheat oven to 375°.

Pare potatoes, cut in ¼-inch slices. Core and cut apples similarly. Butter a 6-cup casserole and arrange slices in alternate layers, sprinkling each layer of potatoes with salt and each layer of apples with sugar. Dot with butter, cover casserole (foil will do), and bake until tender, about 45 minutes. Serves 4–6.

Glazed onions

18–24 small white onions
2 tablespoons butter
½ cup chicken broth or white wine
   Salt, freshly ground pepper
2 teaspoons sugar

Peel onions by dropping into boiling water for about 10 seconds. Drain and run cold water over; skins should slip off easily. Make a cross in the root end of each onion with a sharp knife.

Melt butter in a skillet, add broth and onions, sprinkle salt and pepper over. Cover and simmer very gently for about half an hour, shaking pan occasionally. Uncover, sprinkle with sugar, and cook over medium heat 5 minutes or so, shaking pan frequently until nicely glazed. Serves 4–6.

Creamed onions

Cook as above, but add 2 cups cream sauce (see p. 239) to skillet instead of the sugar and simmer 5 minutes. Serve sprinkled with parsley.

Southern pecan pie

	Basic pastry for a 9-inch pie (see p. 234)
4	eggs
1½	cups dark corn syrup
1	cup sugar
½	teaspoon salt
1	teaspoon vanilla
2–4	tablespoons butter, melted
2	tablespoons dark rum
1½	cups broken pecans
	Whipped cream, optional

Preheat oven to 350°.

Roll out pastry and line a 9-inch pie pan.

Beat eggs in a bowl, then stir in corn syrup, sugar, salt, vanilla, and melted butter.

Place nutmeats on bottom of unbaked pie shell. Pour egg mixture over.

Bake at 350° for 45 minutes, or until filling is set. Serve plain or with whipped cream. Serves 8.

Squash Pie

2	cups squash puree (see note)
2	eggs
2	tablespoons flour
1	teaspoon salt
1½	teaspoons cinnamon
½	teaspoon nutmeg
½	teaspoon allspice
¼	teaspoon ginger
½	cup granulated sugar
½	cup firmly packed dark brown sugar
1	teaspoon vanilla extract
1	Prebaked 9-inch pastry shell (see p. 234)
2	cups milk or light cream

Adjust oven rack to center position, put cookie sheet on it, and preheat oven to 425°.

Beat eggs, add flour, salt, spices, sugars, vanilla, squash puree, and milk. Blend well, pour into prebaked pie crust and bake in a 425° oven for 10 minutes, then reduce heat to 350° and bake 1 hour. Cool on a rack. May be served warm or cold.

Note: About 3 pounds of butternut or Hubbard squash, baked or boiled and put through a food processor will yield about 2 cups. Puree may be made in advance and kept on hand in refrigerator or freezer.

Oyster bisque

½   cup uncooked rice
4   cups chicken broth
4   tablespoons butter
18 oysters, shucked, with their liquid
    Salt, freshly ground black pepper
    Tabasco sauce
1½ cups heavy cream
¼   cup Cognac
    Chopped parsley (optional)

Cook the rice in the broth until very soft. Add the butter. Push the rice through a sieve or whirl in the blender. Finely chop 12 of the oysters or whirl in the blender with their liquid. Add to the rice mixture. Season with salt and pepper to taste and 2–3 dashes Tabasco. Stir in the heavy cream; heat just to the boiling point. Add the 6 whole oysters and heat just until they curl at the edges. Add the Cognac and cook for 2 minutes. Ladle into heated soup cups, putting a whole oyster in each cup. Garnish with chopped parsley if desired. Serves 6. Recipe can be doubled.

CHRISTMAS DAY DINNER

*Oyster bisque

*Baked ham with peaches

*Baked acorn squash

*Green beans with mushrooms

*Cauliflower DuBarry

Watercress, endive and beet salad

*Christmas pudding with brandied hard sauce

Baked ham with peaches

Use a good quality of tenderized ham—not the aged kind and certainly not the tinned kind. Frequent basting is the key to an exceptionally moist and delicious result.

	12–14 pound ham
	Cloves
½	cup orange juice
	Grated zest (colored skin) of 1 large orange or 2 small ones
	Juice from a 1-pound can of peaches
½	cup peach or regular brandy
1	teaspoon ground ginger
1	teaspoon allspice
1	tablespoon dry mustard
	Drained peach halves, currant jam

Preheat oven to 300° (baking schedule: 15 minutes per pound).

Score fat in diamond pattern and stud with cloves. If there is a skin or rind, roll it back for scoring and then back on for roasting. It will be removed later.

Roast 1 hour on a rack in preheated oven.

Remove ham from oven, remove rind, pour orange juice in baking pan, and sprinkle grated orange zest over ham. Return to oven for another hour, basting every 15 minutes.

Mix the brandy and spices into peach juice. Pour entire mixture over ham and continue basting during the remaining cooking time. Raise heat if necessary to get a good mahogany color.

To serve, garnish with drained peach halves filled with a dollop of currant jam.

Baked acorn squash

6   acorn squash of uniform size, washed and dried
        Salt and freshly ground pepper
        Nutmeg
12   teaspoons brown sugar
12   teaspoons butter
12   teaspoons dark rum

Preheat oven to 325°.

Cut squash in half lengthwise, scoop out seeds and fiber, and place, cut side down, on a rimmed cookie sheet. Bake for 25 minutes. Remove from oven, turn halves up, and sprinkle each with salt and pepper. Grate a bit of nutmeg into each cavity, and into each put a teaspoon of butter, one of brown sugar, and a tablespoon of rum. Bake an additional 15–20 minutes or until flesh is tender and easily pierced with a toothpick. Serves 12.

Green beans with mushrooms

2   pounds whole green beans
1   pound fresh mushrooms, stems removed and thinly sliced
4   tablespoons butter
4   tablespoons oil
      Salt and freshly ground pepper

Wash beans and remove tips. Add them a handful at a time to a large pot of boiling, salted water, so that the water does not stop boiling. Cook uncovered 8–10 minutes, then immediately drain and plunge into cold water to stop the cooking. Return beans to empty pot and shake briefly over high heat to dry them. Set aside and keep warm.

Melt the butter in the oil and sauté mushrooms until just wilted. Combine with beans, toss and season well. Serves 8.

Cauliflower DuBarry

2	heads cauliflower
2	cups mashed potatoes
½	cup heavy cream
4	tablespoons butter
	Salt and white pepper
¼	cup grated Gruyère cheese
2	tablespoons butter

Preheat oven to 425°.

Cut cauliflower into florets and cook in boiling salted water until just tender—about 15 minutes. Drain well and puree in a blender or food processor. Mix potatoes and cauliflower puree together, add cream, butter, and salt and pepper to taste. Pile into an ovenproof casserole or gratin dish. Sprinkle top with cheese. Dot with butter, cut in tiny pieces. Bake in upper third of oven for 15 minutes or until top is brown. Serves 12.

Christmas pudding...

(start this in October or early November!)

4	ounces stale white bread
4	ounces suet (preferably beef)
1	pound mixed dried fruit
4	ounces mixed peel
1	small carrot, scraped
1	small apple, peeled
	Juice and grated zest (colored skin) of 1 lemon
1	cup all-purpose flour
2	eggs
1	cup brandy or whiskey
1	teaspoon powdered cinnamon
1	teaspoon mixed spices
2	tablespoons molasses

Mince bread, suet, dried fruit, mixed peel, carrot, and apple. Put in mixing bowl. Add lemon juice and peel. Add flour, eggs, brandy, cinnamon, mixed spices, and molasses and mix thoroughly.

Stir in traditional manner: Each member of the family, with eyes closed and holding the spoon in both hands, stirs the pudding around once while making a wish.

Put in a 6- or 7-cup porcelain pudding basin (not plastic or metal), cover with waxed paper and wrap in foil. Stand in heavy saucepan with hot water halfway up side of the basin, and cover. Steam 6–8 hours. (If halving the mixture or using two basins, steam 3–4 hours).

When cooked, remove covers and then recover tightly and store in a cool place. Wait at least 5 to 6 weeks before using; in any case, the pudding will keep for years if stored in the bottom of a refrigerator.

When needed, boil or steam, as before, for about an hour or more. Serve warm or at room temperature with brandied hard sauce. If desired, when serving this pudding at the table, pour about 2 ounces slightly heated brandy or whiskey around it and ignite. Serves 12.

... with brandied hard sauce

1½ cups fine white sugar
12 tablespoons butter
3   tablespoons brandy or rum, more if desired

Beat sugar and butter together until creamy and light. Add brandy (or rum) fairly slowly, 1 tablespoon at a time. Chill until needed.

CLAMBAKE

An adaptation of the shoreside clambake like the one following first appeared in the 1955 LVIS Cookbook. Instead of the traditional pit dug in the sand or earth, lined with hot rocks and hundreds of pounds of seaweed, it requires an old wash boiler of copper or other metal or even a well-cleaned oil drum. A tight-fitting cover is a necessity, as is enough wet seaweed to fill the container, about 22–25 pounds in the case of a wash boiler.

In the traditional clambake, quartered chickens are cooked along with the other ingredients. For space-saving purposes we suggest you broil or bake them separately in the oven beforehand, or do them on a charcoal grill while the boiler is cooking.

3   3½ pound chickens, quartered, cooked, and kept warm
6   dozen littleneck or cherrystone clams
10 quahog or chowder clams (for flavor only)
    cheesecloth
24 ears of corn, stripped of silk but with husks left on
12 "chicken" lobsters (about 1¼ to 1½ pounds each)
24 new potatoes, skin on
1   pound butter, melted
6   lemons, halved

178 SPECIAL OCCASIONS

Prepare an open fire on the ground, or make a wood fire in a charcoal grill. Use the gas stove as a last resort. Put about 3 inches of water on the bottom of the wash boiler, which should be about 20-gallon capacity. Seawater is marvelous.

Make a package of 6 clams for each person, wrapping them in the cheesecloth. Do not include the quahogs.

Pack the wash boiler with a thick layer of seaweed, and make succeeding layers as follows: clams, seaweed, clams, quahogs, seaweed, corn, seaweed, all the potatoes but one, seaweed, lobsters, seaweed. Put the one potato in the center of the top layer of seaweed. Cover tightly and place on heat. Weight lid down with stones. One-half hour after it boils, check the top potato—if it is tender, the other food should be done. If not, cook a little longer.

Serve each person a chicken quarter, a lobster, a clam package, corn, and potatoes, with melted butter and lemon wedges available. There should also be refuse cans close by for shells, bones, etc. Don't forget the lobster crackers and plenty of paper napkins and cold beer. Watermelon is the traditional topper to this meal. Serves 12.

COVERED-DISH SUPPER

This is a modern version of the old church supper and is still quite popular in East Hampton. Each lady brings a "covered dish"—something she is famous for, or something that feeds a crowd nicely. These are all spread out buffet style on a table; rolls, coffee, and dessert are furnished by the hostess. Some dishes in this book that are ideal for this purpose are:

Salmon mousse
Chicken salad
White bean salad
Manicotti
Salade russe
Baked crab and shrimp
Potato ragout
Chili
Corn pudding

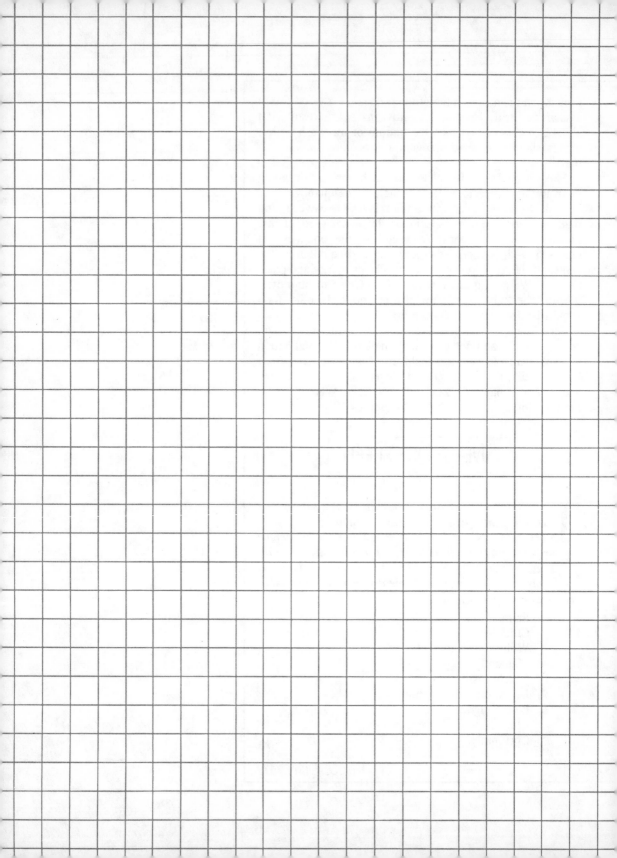

EAST

Food for Drinks & Summertime Parties

HAMPTON

N o effort has been made to organize the food in this section into menus. Having friends in for drinks can mean 4 or 24, and the accepted accompaniments may range from simply nuts and olives or potato chips to finger foods so satisfying that dinner afterward becomes unnecessary.

Crudités ...

(raw vegetables)

In recent years raw vegetables with a savory sauce to dip into have become a classic accompaniment to drinks. Using any number of the following, make an attractive arrangement on a platter and serve one of the suggested dips in a bowl in the center of the platter or alongside. All the vegetables should be as young, fresh, and crisp as possible.

Carrot sticks
Celery sticks
Cucumber sticks
Zucchini sticks (use small tender ones, if   possible)
Cherry tomatoes
Black radishes, cut into paper-thin slices
Red, yellow, or green pepper strips
Red radishes
Small white radishes
Small scallions
Cauliflower florets
Broccoli florets
Asparagus—the pencil-slim size
Raw snow peas
Raw green beans
Sliced mushrooms

... with guacamole

2	large ripe avocados
1	medium tomato, peeled, seeded, and chopped
1	tablespoon finely chopped onion
2–3	serrano or jalapeño chilis (fresh or canned), seeded and finely chopped
	Salt, freshly ground pepper to taste
½	teaspoon lemon juice, or to taste
1	tablespoon finely chopped fresh cilantro (Chinese parsley)

Peel avocados and mash coarsely or pulse a few times in a food processor so some texture remains. (Final dish should not be too smooth.) Add tomato, onion, chilis, salt and pepper to taste, lemon juice, and coriander. Mix well and pile into a serving dish. If you do not plan to serve it immediately, cover well with plastic wrap and refrigerate. Serve as a dip with raw vegetables or taco chips. Makes about 2 cups.

... with curried mayonnaise

1	tablespoon curry powder (or more)
1	teaspoon grated fresh ginger
1	cup mayonnaise, preferably homemade (see Index)
2	tablespoons capers
1	tablespoon each chopped chives and parsley

Mix curry powder and grated ginger into mayonnaise. Blend in capers and chopped chives and parsley. Serve as a dip for vegetables or shrimp. Makes about 1 cup.

... with taramasalata

3	slices white bread (such as Arnold's or Pepperidge Farm), crusts removed
5	ounces tarama (carp roe, available in jars)
2	tablespoons minced onion
1	egg yolk
1	cup olive oil
2	tablespoons lemon juice
2	teaspoons chopped parsley, optional

Crumble bread and soak in ¼ cup water. Put tarama and onion in blender jar and blend until pureed but not liquid. Squeeze out excess water from bread and blend with tarama. Add egg yolk, blend again at medium speed.

Pour in oil in a slow, steady stream as for mayonnaise, then add lemon juice. If the puree seems too liquid, as occasionally happens, add another slice of crustless bread, *unsoaked,* and blend briefly until bread is completely absorbed.

At serving time sprinkle with parsley if desired. Serve as a dip with raw vegetables or with toast, sesame crackers, or Arabic flat bread. Makes about 2½ cups.

... with tapenade

24	pitted black olives
8	anchovy fillets, cut up
1½	tablespoons chopped capers
1	small can tuna fish (3½ ounces)
½	cup oil (half olive, half salad)
3	tablespoons lemon juice
1	garlic clove
1	tablespoon prepared mustard

Put olives, anchovies, capers, and tuna in a blender jar. Puree at low speed. With machine still at low speed, slowly add oil and lemon juice alternately. Put garlic through a press, add, and blend again briefly. Beat in mustard. Add a little more oil if needed to give a smooth consistency like mayonnaise.

Use to dress hard-boiled eggs or as a dip for raw vegetables. Makes about 1 cup.

... with clam dip

1	8-ounce can minced clams or 1 cup of fresh clams, minced
1	3-ounce package cream cheese
1½	teaspoons chopped scallion or onion
½	teaspoon Worcestershire sauce

Drain clams, reserving 1 tablespoon of the clam juice. Soften the cream cheese by beating it with the juice. Add the scallion or onion and the Worcestershire sauce and mix well. Then mix in clams. Serve with crackers, chips, or raw vegetables. Makes about 1–1½ cups.

Homemade "Boursin" cheese

1   8-ounce package cream cheese
2   tablespoons lemon juice
1   large clove garlic
2   shallots
     Fines herbes: ¼ cup parsley, 1 tablespoon chives, 1 teaspoon
     fresh thyme, and 1½ teaspoons fresh tarragon, all very finely
     chopped

Cream the cheese with the lemon juice. Put the garlic and
shallots through a press or mince and add. Add minced herbs.

   Pile into a crock and chill until serving time or mold as
follows: Line an empty 8-ounce margarine tub with plastic
wrap, pile in cheese, and chill. Later remove and peel off
paper to serve. Serve with an unflavored cracker such as
Carr's water crackers.

Note: An easy way to mince herbs is to put them in a small
glass and snip with kitchen scissors.

Sesame cheese sticks

6   slices good sandwich bread, such as Arnold's or Pepperidge
     Farm
     Butter for baking sheet
4   tablespoons unsalted butter, softened
3   tablespoons grated Parmesan cheese
2   teaspoons dried oregano
1   clove garlic, put through a press
     Salt
3   tablespoons sesame seeds

186   FOOD FOR DRINKS AND SUMMERTIME PARTIES

Freeze the bread. Butter a baking sheet.

Mix butter, cheese, oregano, garlic, and a dash of salt, and beat briefly. Add the sesame seeds and mix well to make a smooth paste. Spread the frozen bread with paste. Cut each slice into 6 strips and put on baking sheet. Bake in a 275° oven 45–60 minutes. Check them after 30 minutes, and move about a bit if browning too fast.

Remove from oven, cool on cake racks, and store in a glass jar. These keep indefinitely.

Marinated shrimp

¾	cup olive oil
3	cloves garlic, minced
1	small onion, minced
2	pounds raw shrimp, shelled and deveined
6	scallions, minced (white and part of green)
½	cup wine vinegar
1	teaspoon salt
1	teaspoon dry mustard
¼	teaspoon cayenne

Heat ¼ cup of the oil in a large heavy skillet. Sauté garlic and onion over moderate heat until transparent, stirring constantly, about 8–10 minutes.

Add shrimp to skillet, raise heat a bit, and cook 5–7 minutes, always stirring, until they turn pink. Remove from heat and cool. Make marinade of remaining oil, scallions, vinegar, mustard, cayenne, and salt in a large bowl. Add shrimp, toss thoroughly, and chill several hours or overnight. Stir them up occasionally.

Serve in a bowl placed in a larger one filled with cracked ice. Mask ice with bunches of parsley. This recipe may be easily doubled. Serves 8 with drinks, or 4 as a first course.

Marinated scallops

1   pound scallops
        Juice of 2 limes
2   tablespoons chopped dill

Marinate scallops in the lime juice and chopped dill for
3–4 hours in the refrigerator. Serve with toothpicks.

Shrimp spread

3   3-ounce packages cream cheese
1   pound shrimp, cooked, cleaned, and peeled
3   tablespoons chili sauce
2   tablespoons grated onion
1   teaspoon Worcestershire sauce
1   tablespoon lemon juice
        Milk
¼   cup chopped walnuts
2   tablespoons chopped parsley

Mash cheese with a fork and whip until very smooth.
Chop shrimp very fine and blend in. Add chili sauce,
onion, Worcestershire, and lemon juice, and blend in. If
mixture seems too stiff, beat in some milk, 1 teaspoon at a
time, until a pleasing consistency is reached.

   Pack into a serving bowl or crock, and chill. Just before
serving, mix nuts and parsley and mask top of spread.
Serve with crackers for spreading.

Clam Fritters

1½   cups flour
½   teaspoon salt
8   tablespoons (1 stick) butter
3   eggs, separated
¾   cup beer
24   fresh cherrystone clams
1   tablespoon parsley, finely chopped
1   tablespoon snipped chives
      Lemon wedges
      Parsley sprigs

Put flour and salt in a mixing bowl. Melt 4 tablespoons of the butter and add. Beat the egg yolks lightly and add. Gradually blend in the beer and let this batter stand in a warm place for 1 hour.

Chop the clams fine and add them, with the parsley and chives, to the batter. Beat the egg whites until stiff, stir a small amount into the batter, and then fold the rest in.

Heat the remaining butter in a heavy skillet. When hot, drop in the batter by spoonfuls. Brown the fritters lightly on both sides and drain on paper towels. Serve hot, as hors d'oeuvres or as a first course, garnished with lemon wedges and parsley. Makes about thirty-six 2½-inch fritters.

Horseradish shrimp sandwiches

1   pound cooked shrimp
1   teaspoon prepared mustard
1   tablespoon mayonnaise
2   teaspoons prepared horseradish, or more to taste
1   tablespoon chopped chives
      Lemon juice
      Whipped cream
      Salt and pepper to taste
16   thin slices bread

Peel and clean shrimp. Chop very fine by hand or in a food processor. Add mustard, mayonnaise, horseradish, chives, a few drops of lemon juice, and enough whipped cream to bind and give a good spreading consistency. Season to taste with salt and pepper. Remove crusts from bread and make sandwiches. Cut each into 4 triangles. Makes about 36 small sandwiches.

Cheese puffs

1   3-ounce package cream cheese
1   egg yolk
2   tablespoons grated onion
      Cayenne pepper
12   slices good white bread

Cream the cheese and unbeaten egg yolk. Add grated onion and a dash of red pepper.

Preheat oven to 450° and cut 2 rounds per slice from the bread. Put about a teaspoon of cheese mixture on rounds and bake on a cookie sheet 8–10 minutes. Makes about 24.

Hommus

(chick-pea–sesame dip)

1   cup canned chick-peas, drained
⅓   cup lemon juice, or more to taste
4   tablespoons tahini (see note) beaten into ½ cup water
2   garlic cloves
    Salt and freshly ground pepper to taste
    Paprika

Put chick-peas, lemon juice, and tahini mixture in a food processor. Put garlic cloves through a press and add. Blend until thick and creamy. Season to taste. Pile into a serving bowl, sprinkle paprika on top, and serve with unsalted crackers or crisp pita bread (see Index). Makes about 2 cups.

Note: Tahini, or sesame seed butter, is available in jars in food specialty shops.

Bacon-broiled clams

4   dozen littleneck clams
½   cup chopped scallions (including green part)
10 slices bacon, cut into 48 pieces to fit shells

Preheat broiler. Open clams (or have them opened). Place 48 shells on a large rimmed baking pan. Put a clam on each shell. Sprinkle with scallions and place a piece of bacon on top of each. Broil under hot broiler just until bacon is browned, 3–5 minutes. Serve at once with crusty bread for mopping up the pan juices. Serves 4 as a first course, 12 with drinks.

Striped bass appetizer

1   3-pound striped bass, filleted with skin reserved
½   cup corn oil
1   teaspoon salt
1   small bay leaf
      Juice of 1 lemon
      Cocktail sauce

Put 2 quarts water in a fish poacher and add the oil, salt, bay leaf, and lemon juice. Add the reserved fish skins. Bring to a boil, then remove from heat.

Trim off dark meat from fillets and discard. Add fillets to poaching liquid, cover, bring to a second boil, lower heat, and poach gently 3–5 minutes, depending on thickness. Remove from liquid and cool on a plate. Then refrigerate.

To serve, cut into bite-size pieces and pass with cocktail sauce. Even nonfish-eaters like this one. Serves 8 with drinks.

Cherrystone clams with garlic

For each person put 12 cherrystone clams on a large square of heavy-duty aluminum foil. In a small bowl put enough salt to equal about ¼ teaspoon per person. Add a generous amount of freshly ground black pepper and one peeled and smashed garlic clove per person. Mix this seasoning well and sprinkle over clams. Add a good lump of butter. Bring foil up over clams and twist to make a tight bundle. Put on a medium-hot charcoal fire and cook 8–10 minutes, shaking packages once or twice. Open one package to test—clams should be removed from fire the minute they are open. Serve each person a clam bundle with hot French bread to dunk in the tasty sauce.

Pissaladière

This savory onion tart could be considered a southern French cousin of the pizza. It is nice as a first course, served either at the table or with predinner drinks.

3   large onions, finely chopped
3   tablespoons butter
3   tablespoons olive oil
     Salt, finely ground pepper
1   recipe cream cheese pastry (see p. 233)
     Anchovy fillets
     Black Italian-style olives (oil cured), pitted

Preheat oven to 425°.

Sauté the onions in the butter and oil for 3 minutes, but do not let them brown. Cover and steam until soft and tender. Season with salt and pepper to taste.

Roll out the dough ¼-inch thick and lay out on a baking sheet. Using a 9- or 10-inch plate as a guide, cut a circle of the dough and remove the excess. Spread the steamed onions over the dough circle and arrange a lattice of anchovy fillets on top, putting a black olive in the spaces between the fillets. Bake for 10 minutes, then reduce heat to 375° and bake 20–25 minutes longer. Cut into wedges and serve warm or at room temperature. Serves 6–8 with drinks.

Clams on the half shell

Whether littlenecks or cherrystones, clams on the half shell taste best icy cold. Have them opened at the market and keep refrigerated until the last minute. To serve, place a good layer of chopped ice on a metal tray or a jelly roll pan and cover with a kitchen towel. This will keep the melting water from getting into the clams. Arrange the clams on the half shell in a single layer. Have a bowl of cocktail sauce, lemon wedges, and a pepper grinder nearby and an empty bowl or wastebasket for the shells. Clam lovers can demolish a half dozen in the blink of an eye, so plan on at least this number per guest and replenish the tray from the refrigerator at intervals.

Mussels remoulade

2	quarts mussels
1	cup dry white wine
3	cloves garlic, peeled
½	cup mayonnaise
2	teaspoons dry mustard
3	dashes Tabasco
6	small scallions, minced (white and part of green)
1	tablespoon minced parsley
	Salt to taste
	Paprika (optional)

Rinse mussels well, scrub and debeard them. Put them in a heavy pot or pan with the white wine and garlic cloves, cover and steam 8–10 minutes or until open. Remove and let cool. (Discard any that remain closed.)

Make a sauce by mixing the mayonnaise, mustard, tabasco, scallions, parsley, and lemon juice, and salt to taste. Remove mussels from shells, reserving half of them. Stir mussels into sauce to coat well and put one back into each shell with a little of the sauce. Dust tops lightly with paprika if desired. Chill until serving time. Pass on a tray as a drink accompaniment or serve on a bed of shredded lettuce as a first course.

Kielbasa vinaigrette

1   large Polish kielbasa sausage
        Red wine
1   medium onion, thinly sliced
5–6   scallions, thinly sliced (the white and some of the green)
¼   cup finely chopped parsley
1   ripe tomato, peeled, seeded and cut in thin strips
½   cup mustard vinaigrette (see p. 237)

Poach the sausage as follows: Put sausage in an enameled or stainless steel skillet, cover with a mixture of half red wine and half water, and add onion slices. Bring to the boil, cover, lower heat, and cook gently 20–30 minutes. Cool in the poaching liquid.

When cool enough to handle, carefully remove the skin and slice thin. Toss in a salad bowl with the scallions, parsley, and tomato. Add the vinaigrette sauce, toss again and let stand at least an hour. As an hors d'oeuvre serve with toothpicks.

Can also be served on a bed of lettuce as a first course.

New potatoes with caviar

Gather tiny small new potatoes, the smaller the better. Those gleaned just after the harvester has passed through a Long Island potato field taste best of all. Scrub and bake with skins on, in a preheated 350° oven, until soft. Cut in half, top each half with a dollop of sour cream, then an appropriate amount of red caviar, and a few snipped chives on top. Arrange on a plate and serve while still warm.

Chopped chicken liver spread

1	large onion, chopped
	Rendered chicken fat (below)
1	pound chicken livers, washed, dried, and cut up
4	hard-cooked eggs
	Salt, freshly ground pepper
	Chopped cracklings, optional

Sauté onion in chicken fat until golden. Remove from pan and set aside. Sauté livers quickly until they just lose their red color. Overcooking makes them tough and bitter.

Chop the eggs fine and put into a bowl. If you have rendered your own chicken fat and have cracklings, dry them out a bit in a slow oven and chop fine. Chop livers and, using 2 forks, mix with onions and cracklings, salt and pepper to taste, and enough chicken fat to bind. Pack into a crock or bowl and chill. Serve with melba toast. Makes about 3 cups.

RENDERED CHICKEN FAT:

1 pound raw chicken fat in lumps plus any fatty skin
2 small onions, diced

Place fat in heavy skillet. Cover fat with cold water. Bring
to the boil, cover, lower heat, and simmer covered for
about 20 minutes. Uncover and cook over low heat until
fat is melted and water is evaporated. Add onion, cooking
until golden to flavor the fat. Strain fat and refrigerate.

Note: The browned bits of skin and onions that are left
over when rendering chicken fat are called cracklings.
Some people like to eat them as is, as a nibble. They add a
very good flavor when chopped and added to chopped
liver spread.

Sausage biscuits

1   pound country sausage meat
10 ounces sharp coon cheese, grated
3   cups Bisquick

Combine sausage, cheese, and Bisquick thoroughly to make
dough. Make into bite-size balls and bake on a cookie
sheet for 20 minutes in a 375° oven. Serve piping hot.
Makes about 120 small biscuits.

Note: The uncooked balls may be frozen for future use.

Steak tartare Salzburg

2   pounds very freshly ground lean beef, ground twice
1   2-ounce tin flat anchovies, drained, very finely chopped, oil reserved
       Salt, freshly ground black pepper
       Cayenne pepper
2   tablespoons Worcestershire sauce
1   tablespoon prepared mustard
3   tablespoons capers
1   tablespoon olive oil from anchovy can
1   small onion, very finely minced
2   tablespoons parsley
2   raw egg yolks

Mix all ingredients in a bowl. Turn out on a board and chop together very fine. Mound onto a serving platter, garnish with more chopped parsley if desired, and serve surrounded by a variety of bread in small squares or rounds. Serves 12 with drinks.

Eggplant orientale

Prepare recipe for eggplant orientale (see p. 94) but chop eggplant in fine dice instead of coarsely. Put in chilled serving bowl and garnish lavishly with fresh dill. Serve with thin, well-buttered slices of black bread. Serves 8 to 10 for cocktails.

Grilled flank steak sandwiches

This idea for a hearty drink accompaniment came from James Beard.

2	flank steaks (London broil)
1	cup dry red wine
½	cup salad oil
1	clove garlic, chopped
1	onion, sliced
½	cup chopped parsley
	Salt and freshly ground pepper
2	medium-size loaves French bread
	Butter at room temperature
1	clove garlic, pressed
¼	teaspoon thyme

Remove the tough outer membrane from the meat. Put the wine, oil, chopped garlic, sliced onion, and parsley in a shallow bowl. Let the meat marinate at least 3 hours, or better, overnight, in the refrigerator. Turn meat several times while marinating. Keep refrigerated until last minute before grilling.

When coals are very hot, grill meat quickly. Have grill close enough to coals to cook steak crusty brown on outside and rare in center in 4 minutes per side. (This is a cut that must not be well done.) Brush meat with marinade while cooking and season with salt and pepper.

In the meantime, prepare the bread: Split loaves the long way. Mix butter with the garlic—a lot or little, as you prefer—and thyme and spread on each half. Put loaves together again, wrap in foil, and heat on back of grill or in oven before starting steak.

When steak is ready, remove to a cutting board and with a very sharp knife cut in thin diagonal slices. Place on the lengths of bread. You can make open-faced sandwiches or cover with another length of bread, as you choose. Cut crosswise in a convenient size. Serves 20–25 as an hors d'oeuvre.

Herb canapés

1	tablespoon sesame seeds
1	egg
¼	pound butter, softened
1	tablespoon flour
¼	teaspoon marjoram
¼	teaspoon basil
¼	teaspoon rosemary
1	tablespoon minced chives or scallions
	Toasted rounds or squares of bread

Toast sesame seeds by heating in a dry skillet until they begin to pop and color. Mix with egg, butter, flour, and herbs and spread on toasted bread rounds or squares. Put on a cookie sheet and bake in a 350° oven until top bubbles. Makes about 2 dozen.

French-fried zucchini

6–8	young zucchini
	Salt
½	cup flour
	Freshly ground pepper
	Oil for deep frying

Cut unpeeled zucchini into narrow strips, the size of thin french fries. Spread them on tea towels, sprinkle with salt, and let stand about an hour. Pat dry with paper towels. Put flour and pepper to taste in a paper bag and shake the strips in it, to coat them. Heat fat to 365° and fry a small batch at a time until golden, keeping each batch warm in the oven. Drain strips on paper towels, sprinkle with additional salt if needed, and keep hot to retain crispness.

Serve with cocktails or as a vegetable with a main course. Serves 4–6 as a vegetable, 8–10 with drinks.

Cocktail pecans

4	teaspoons Worcestershire sauce
2	teaspoons Lowry's seasoned salt
6	tablespoons butter
1	pound whole large pecan halves

Melt the butter in a skillet and add the Worcestershire sauce and the seasoned salt. Add pecan halves to skillet and turn with a spoon to coat them with butter mixture. Turn out on a rimmed baking sheet and bake in a 275° oven for 45 minutes, stirring two or three times. The nuts should be dry and fairly dark at the end. These nuts can be kept for a very long time in a tightly covered glass or plastic container.

Miniature croque-monsieur

Make a croque-monsieur according to the regular recipe (see Index). Trim off the crusts and cut into 4 triangles. Pass while hot. Six regular sandwiches will yield 24 miniatures.

EAST HAMPTON

Pickles, Preserves, & Relishes

Hot pepper jelly

A hot accompaniment to lamb or beef.

1	cup green pepper, seeded and minced
½	cup jalapeño peppers, seeded and minced
1½	cups cider vinegar
6½	cups granulated sugar
1	6-ounce bottle liquid pectin

Combine peppers, vinegar, and sugar and bring to a boil. Boil 5–7 minutes, then skim foam twice, off heat. Stir in liquid pectin and pour into sterilized jars. Will keep refrigerated indefinitely, without a wax seal. Makes 6 pints.

Green tomato pickle

This is a good way to use green tomatoes just before frost, and is a pleasant accompaniment to roasts or ham.

6	pounds green tomatoes
3	pounds small white onions, peeled
	Salt
1	quart white vinegar
6	cloves
3	pounds light brown sugar
4	tablespoons mustard seed
2	tablespoons celery seed
1	tablespoon turmeric

Slice tomatoes and onions thin; soak for 1½ hours in brine made of ¼ cup salt to 2 quarts water. Put vinegar and seasonings into a large deep pot, bring to a boil and boil for 10 minutes. Drain tomatoes and onions and add. Bring again to a boil, lower heat and simmer, uncovered, until tomatoes are tender enough to be pierced with a straw and have become rather dark.

Pour into sterilized jars and seal while hot. Makes about 9 pints.

Rhubarb Jelly

> About 2 pounds rhubarb, green or pink
> Sugar
> ½ bottle liquid pectin (Certo)
> Imitation strawberry flavoring, optional

Slice rhubarb but do not pull strings. Put in a pot, barely cover with water, bring to a boil, cover pot, and simmer until soft and tender. Put fruit through a sieve or a food mill, then strain the puree through a jelly cloth or a folded cheesecloth. Measure the juice carefully, then measure out exactly double that amount in sugar.

Combine the rhubarb puree, juice, and sugar in a kettle and bring to a boil, stirring constantly. Stir in the Certo, bring to a hard rolling boil, and boil 2½–3 minutes, again stirring constantly. Make the jelly test (see Index).

If the rhubarb is pale, 1 or 2 drops of imitation strawberry flavoring can be used for color. It is added at the same time as the liquid pectin.

Remove from heat, skim foam, if any, and pour quickly into prepared sterilized jelly glasses. Cover at once with ⅛ inch hot paraffin.

Beach plum jelly I

Mrs. E. J. Edwards
The 60th Anniversary Book

Wash beach plums. Pit, and barely cover with water and cook until very soft. Strain through cheesecloth, pressing lightly, until juice has dripped through. Put juice in an enameled saucepan and bring to a boil. Boil until reduced by half.

Measure the juice and return to the pot. Add 1 cup of sugar for each cup of beach plum juice. Boil a few minutes until jelly "sheets" (see p. 211: "Some jelly- and jam-making hints").

Pour into sterilized jelly glasses set in a pan of hot water. When cool, pour melted paraffin on top of each glass.

Beach plum jelly II

3	cups pitted beach plums
3	cups sugar
1	cup water
1	cup tart apples, peeled, cored, and chopped

Bring all ingredients to a boil in a 3-quart saucepan; lower heat and continue cooking for about 20 minutes or until a candy thermometer registers 220°–222° or until jelly "sheets" (see p. 211: "Some jelly- and jam-making hints").

Place mixture in a paper coffee cone filter or a strainer lined with cheesecloth and let it drip through (this will take about half an hour). Pour the resulting liquid into sterilized jars or refrigerate. Yield: 1–1½ cups jelly.

Note: The fruit left in the cone is beach plum conserve, and makes a pleasant accompaniment to meat. If it is too thick, add a little boiling water; you will have about 1½ cups.

Bread-and-butter pickles

20	medium-size cucumbers, or enough to make 6 quarts when sliced
20	small white onions peeled, enough to make 2 quarts when sliced
2½	green peppers, stemmed and seeded
½	cup coarse salt
1	quart cracked ice

Wash cucumbers and remove stem and blossom ends. Slice into ¼-inch slices. Slice white onions thin and slice green peppers into thin rings. Put in a large bowl and mix with salt and ice. Cover and weight. Let stand for 3 hours. Drain well and mix with a dressing made of the following ingredients:

4½–5	cups sugar
1½	teaspoons turmeric
½	teaspoon ground cloves
2	tablespoons yellow mustard seeds
1	tablespoon celery seed
4½–5	cups cider vinegar

Combine dressing ingredients in a large kettle and let simmer until well blended. Add cucumbers, onions, and pepper, and simmer until the skins turn just a little brown—about 10 minutes. Do not boil.

Cool slightly, fill sterilized pint jars, and seal. Makes about 8 pints.

Three-fruit marmalade

1	grapefruit
2	oranges
2	lemons
	Sugar
	Grand Marnier or Cointreau

This marmalade is made over a period of three days, is extremely pungent and not bitter.

Quarter grapefruit, oranges, and lemons. Using a very sharp knife, remove all seeds and slice the fruit carefully into paper-thin slices. Measure the fruit in a Pyrex cup measure and put in a bowl. Cover it with 3 times its measure of water. Let soak overnight.

Next day, cook over high heat for 20 minutes. Put back into the bowl to cool for 24 hours.

On the third day, measure the fruit and liquid carefully. Then measure out ¾ cup sugar for each cup of fruit and juice. If you warm the sugar as described in "Some jelly- and jam-making hints" (see p. 211), it will dissolve more rapidly and shorten cooking time. Divide fruit mixture into 2 smaller pots and cook for about half an hour or until one of the jelly tests also described in "Hints" is successful, or 220°–222° is reached on a candy thermometer. Watch carefully during the cooking, stir frequently to avoid scorching. Mixture will froth while cooking.

Off heat, add the juice of ½ lemon to each pot and a good slosh of Grand Marnier or Cointreau. Pour into sterilized jars and seal. Makes about 3 pints marmalade.

Strawberry Preserves

PROPORTIONS:
1   cup firm berries
1¾   cup sugar

Crush berries slightly. Cook with sugar on a low fire until sugar dissolves. After boiling point is reached, allow to boil slowly:

8   minutes for 1 quart
10   minutes for 2 quarts

Don't cook more than 2 quarts at a time. Pour into a large bowl, stir from time to time. Let stand overnight in a cool place. (If too much syrup appears to have formed, drain off and reserve for flavoring summer drinks, or use as an ice-cream topping.) Put in sterilized jars and seal well with wax or paraffin.

Cranberry Sauce

Cook 1 pound of cranberries with 2 cups of water in an uncovered saucepan, until berries begin to pop. Sweeten to taste with 1–2 cups sugar. Off the heat, stir in the grated zest (colored skin) of 1 orange and 2 tablespoons Grand Marnier or Cointreau.

This sauce keeps for at least 10 days in the refrigerator.

Spiced pear butter

7	quarts cut-up pears (Bartlett, Bosc)
1	cup red wine
½	cup white vinegar
5–6	sticks cinnamon
2	tablespoons whole cloves
2	cups sugar
¼	cup lemon juice
½	cup orange juice
¼	teaspoon allspice

Cook pears with wine, vinegar, cinnamon, and cloves over medium heat until pears are soft, about 10 minutes. Put through a food mill and return puree to a heavy pot. (See note.)

Add sugar, lemon juice, orange juice, and allspice, and stir. Cook over low heat for 1 hour until thickened. Watch for scorching. Makes about 5 pints.

Note: You should have about 8 cups of puree at this point. However, depending on size and juiciness of pears, this will vary. Amounts of sugar, juices, and allspice are based on 8 cups and so may have to be adjusted slightly.

Cranberry-orange relish

Mrs. F. Milliken
The 60th Anniversary Book

Put 1 pound of cranberries and a whole orange through the meat grinder. Sweeten to taste (about 2 cups sugar) and refrigerate for 24 hours before serving.

Some jelly- and jam-making hints

Preheat your sugar by spreading it in a baking pan and putting it in a 250° for 15 minutes. This quickens dissolving time.

Don't hesitate to make several batches; the best flavor comes when you work in small quantities.

Use porcelain or stainless steel pots when making jams and jellies.

CLASSICAL JELLY TEST ("SHEETING"):
Spoon up a small amount of the jelly, let it cool a bit, and then drop it back into the pot from the side of the spoon. As it thickens, two big drops will appear along spoon edge. When the two come together and drop as one, this is equal to 220° on a candy thermometer.

SAUCER TEST:
Several hours before starting a jam, jelly, or preserve, put several saucers in the refrigerator to chill. To see if proper jelling point has been reached, put a spoonful of hot jelly on a chilled saucer. Put saucer back in refrigerator for 5 minutes or so, by which time liquid should have jelled. If you can then make jelly run by tilting saucer, it needs more cooking. Test again at frequent intervals.

Start testing before you think it's done, because over-cooking tends to make jams, etc., become rubbery.

Don't change the proportions of sugar to pectin stated in a given recipe.

Peach chutney

4	cups peeled, pitted, and chopped peaches (about 3 pounds)
¾	cup vinegar
¼	cup lemon juice
1	cup raisins
⅓	cup chopped onion
2	cloves garlic, minced
¼	cup chopped fresh ginger or drained and slivered preserved ginger
1	tablespoon salt
1	teaspoon allspice
½	teaspoon cinnamon
½	teaspoon ground cloves
½	teaspoon ground ginger
7½	cups (3¼ pounds) sugar
1	bottle liquid pectin

Put the peaches into a large kettle and add the vinegar, lemon juice, raisins, onion, garlic, salt and spices.

Add the sugar and mix thoroughly. Put over high heat and bring to a rolling boil, stirring occasionally. Boil hard 1 minute, stirring constantly.

Remove from heat and stir in the pectin immediately. Skim off the foam with a metal spoon and stir and skim for 5 minutes to cool slightly and prevent floating fruit. Ladle into hot, sterilized jelly glasses; and pour a ⅛-inch layer of melted paraffin wax over each glass. Store in a cool, dry, dark place.

Makes about 2½ quarts or 10–12 jelly glasses. Particularly good with meats.

EAST

Breads & Pastries

HAMPTON

Hans Namuth's bread

Photographer Hans Namuth has a house in Watermill and is the undisputed dean of home bakers in the area. He is famous for the bread below, which he makes each weekend. His suggestion (not calculated to endear him to women's lib) is that as this is a man's recipe, women might halve it for easier handling.

4	packets yeast
1	teaspoon sugar
4	cups warm water
8	cups or more unbleached white flour
2	tablespoons honey
½	cup coarse salt
2	tablespoons melted butter or 4 ounces plain yogurt
3	tablespoons wheat germ
	Cornmeal
¼	cup olive oil

Sprinkle yeast and sugar over 2 cups of warm water (see notes) in a warmed bowl. Stir gently. Let stand 30 minutes, or until surface is bubbly. Add 2 cups of the flour and beat with a wooden spoon until smooth. Stir in 4 or more cups of flour and the balance of the water, and when you have a cohesive mass, start kneading in the bowl. Then turn dough onto a lightly floured board or counter and with more flour at hand, continue kneading for about 10 minutes, adding additional flour as necessary. (The exact amount of flour to be added at this point varies with the weather: Mr. Namuth has used up to 10 cups [5 pounds] total, on occasion.)

Form dough into a ball and put it into a bowl large enough for it to double comfortably. Sprinkle with flour. Cover with a clean tea towel and let rise in a warm place for 2 hours until doubled in size (see notes).

Punch dough down a couple of times and add the honey,

salt, melted butter or yogurt, and the wheat germ; work these in with the hands. Add more flour if necessary.

Again, form into a ball, sprinkle with flour, put into the bowl, and cover with the towel and let rise a second time in a warm place. Punch down and cut into 4 equal portions. Form into round or long loaves as you prefer.

Prepare two baking sheets by lining them with waxed paper and sprinkling them with cornmeal. Put 2 loaves on each, sprinkle with flour, and cover each with a clean tea towel to rise for the third time. (This rising will take less time than the others, about 1½ hours.)

Preheat oven to 350° for 15 minutes. Slash each loaf in 3 places with a razor, about ½ inch deep, and brush on olive oil. Bake 60–70 minutes, turning the pans at least twice during that time. If you wish a very crusty bread, raise oven temperature to 550° for last 10 minutes.

Bread is done when it sounds hollow when rapped on bottom. If you are uncertain, break off a little piece to taste: if too moist, bake a little longer.

Brush excess cornmeal off loaves and cool them on a rack.

Wrapped in heavy-duty foil, this bread freezes very well.

Makes 4 loaves.

Variation: After third rising, instead of brushing with olive oil, brush with beaten egg yolk and sprinkle on sesame seeds.

Notes: Water for dissolving yeast should be between 105° and 115°. If in doubt, use a meat or candy thermometer.

A "warm place" is one that is draft free and has a temperature of around 75°–80°. Inside the oven with just the pilot light on is a good place.

Dough is properly kneaded when it is satiny, smooth and elastic, and no longer sticks to your hands.

If you are not sure if dough has doubled, press two fingers in the center. If the dent remains, it has doubled.

A metal spatula is helpful in scraping up bits of dough that adhere to the work surface.

Dill bread

2¼–2½ cups flour
1   package active dry yeast
2   tablespoons sugar
1   tablespoon minced onion
2   teaspoons dill seeds or chopped fresh dill
1   teaspoon salt
¼   teaspoon baking soda
1   cup creamed cottage cheese
1   tablespoon butter
1   egg, lightly beaten
     Butter
     Coarse salt

Combine 1 cup flour with the yeast, sugar, onion, dill seeds, salt, and soda.

Heat the cottage cheese in butter in a small saucepan until lukewarm, and add to the flour mixture. Add the egg and blend well. Beat in the remaining flour.

Cover and let rise in a warm place 50–60 minutes or until doubled in bulk. Butter a 2-quart casserole. Stir down dough, turn into casserole and let rise again 30–40 minutes. Preheat oven to 350° and bake 40–45 minutes, until golden brown. Brush with melted butter and sprinkle with coarse salt.

Cool in casserole for 15 minutes, then turn out on a wire rack to cool completely. This bread also makes delicious melba toast.

Pumpkin bread

	Butter for pans
4	eggs
1	cup cooking oil
⅔	cup water
1	16-ounce can unsweetened pumpkin pie filling or 2 cups puree (see note)
3½	cups sifted flour
2⅔	cups sugar
2	teaspoons baking soda
½	teaspoon baking powder
1½	teaspoons salt
1	teaspoon cinnamon
1	teaspoon nutmeg
½	teaspoon powdered cloves
⅔	cup chopped walnuts
⅔	cup chopped raisins

Butter two 8½- × 4½- × 2½-inch loaf pans.

Preheat oven to 350°.

Beat eggs, add and mix in oil and water. Stir in the pumpkin puree. Mix together and sift the flour, sugar, baking soda, baking powder, salt, and spices, then stir this into pumpkin mixture, using wire whisk. Add nuts and raisins and mix well. Pour into prepared loaf pans. Bake 55–65 minutes, until a straw or toothpick inserted in center comes out clean. If straw or toothpick comes out moist on testing, check in another 5 minutes. Breads should be moist. Cool on racks in the pans; remove when cool. These breads refrigerate and freeze well if wrapped in plastic wrap or foil.

Note: If using fresh pumpkin puree, increase sugar to 3 cups.

Banana-orange muffins

(a lo-cal bread)

Butter for muffin tins
1½ cups flour
1½ teaspoons granulated sugar substitute
1 tablespoon baking powder
¼ teaspoon salt
1 cup wheat germ
1 cup mashed bananas (about 2 medium ripe bananas)
½ cup orange juice
¼ cup cooking oil
2 eggs, lightly beaten

Preheat oven to 400°. Butter or paper-line muffin tins.

Sift together flour, sugar substitute, baking powder, and salt. Stir in wheat germ. Combine bananas, orange juice, oil, and eggs in a separate bowl. Make a well in center of dry ingredients and pour in banana mixture.

Stir just until dry ingredients are moistened; do not overmix. Fill tins ⅔ full and bake at 400° 20–25 minutes or until golden brown. Makes 18 muffins.

Hush puppies

Hush puppies are said to date back to the early 1700s and were often used by colonial settlers while out hunting to silence howling hounds—hence the name. Eventually they evolved as an accompaniment to fish dishes on shooting-party menus.

2   cups cornmeal
½   teaspoon baking soda
1   teaspoon salt
1   teaspoon baking powder
1   tablespoon flour
1   teaspoon chopped onion
1   cup buttermilk
1   whole egg, beaten
       Oil for frying

Mix dry ingredients together. Add onion, then buttermilk, and lastly the egg. Drop by the spoonful into a pan or kettle, in which fish is being fried. Fry to golden brown, drain on paper. If a deep kettle is being used, the hush puppy breads will float when done.

Popovers

1   cup sifted all-purpose flour
¼   teaspoon salt
¾   cup plus 2 tablespoons milk
2   eggs
1   tablespoon melted butter
       Butter for pan

Sift flour and salt together and gradually add milk, beating with a wooden spoon to make a smooth batter. Beat eggs until light and add to butter. Add the melted butter and beat vigorously.

Preheat oven to 45°. Butter 9 holes of a muffin pan or an equal number of custard cups.

Let muffin pan or custard cups heat in the oven for 5 minutes. Then fill ⅔ full with batter and bake for 30 minutes. Lower heat to 350° and bake 10 minutes longer. Makes 9.

Blueberry pancakes

1⅓	cups flour
2	teaspoons baking powder
1	tablespoon sugar
¼	teaspoon salt
2	eggs
⅔	cup milk
2	tablespoons melted butter
¾–1	cup blueberries
	Butter for griddle

Combine flour, baking powder, sugar, and salt in a small bowl. In a large bowl beat eggs and add milk and butter. Beat flour mixture into egg mixture and blend well, but leave some lumps. Let batter rest 20–30 minutes. Then fold in berries, being careful not to mash them.

Heat griddle and butter it as necessary for each batch of pancakes. Serve with maple syrup. Serves 4.

Swedish pancakes

2	cups all-purpose flour
1	teaspoon salt
2	tablespoons sugar
3	cups milk
4	eggs, lightly beaten
2	tablespoons melted butter
½	cup heavy cream, whipped

Sift together the flour, salt, and sugar. Add the milk to the beaten eggs in a mixing bowl, then slowly blend in the flour mixture. Add melted butter. It is essential to let this batter stand for at least 2 hours.

Make thin pancakes as follows: Heat a small amount of butter in a 7-inch skillet. Pour in a small amount of batter and tilt pan so bottom is covered evenly. When bubbles appear, turn pancake and cook other side. Add butter as needed, and continue making pancakes in this manner. Turn them out into a buttered Pyrex dish as they are done, and keep warm. To serve, spread each with strawberry jam and stack them into a cake. Top with whipped cream. Cut in wedges as a regular cake. Serves 6–8.

Tansy pancakes

An old-fashioned spring tonic

2	eggs
1	cup milk
½	cup molasses
2	cups flour
1	teaspoon cream of tartar
½	teaspoon soda
	Pinch of salt
2	tablespoons melted butter
½	cup tansy–the tansy must be young sprigs in the spring, not more than 1"–1½"

Sift together cream of tartar, soda, salt, and flour into bowl. Mix egg yolks with milk and molasses. Combine flour mixture with liquids, stir in melted butter and chopped tansy. Fold in beaten egg whites. Bake on griddle as regular pancakes, serve with plenty of butter and syrup.

Date-nut bread

This bread has a special affinity for cream cheese.

	Butter for pan
1½	cups boiling water
1	cup pitted dates, cut up coarsely
2	cups flour
1	teaspoon baking powder
1	teaspoon baking soda
½	teaspoon salt
½	cup chopped pecans
2	eggs
1	cup brown sugar, firmly packed
2	tablespoons butter, melted

Preheat oven to 350°.

Butter an 8½- × 4½- × 2½-inch loaf pan.

Pour boiling water over dates and let stand for 10 minutes.

Sift flour with baking powder, soda, and salt; stir in nuts. Beat the eggs with the sugar in a separate bowl. Add the melted butter to the dates.

Add the dry ingredients and the date mixture to the egg mixture alternately, blending well after each addition.

Pour into prepared loaf pan and bake 1 hour. Cool on a rack.

Buttermilk pound cake

This pound cake, less dense than most, is tasty and moist.

8	ounces sweet butter (2 sticks)
2	cups granulated sugar
4	eggs (at room temperature)
1	teaspoon vanilla
2	tablespoons lemon juice
3	cups flour
½	teaspoon baking soda
½	teaspoon baking powder
¾	teaspoon salt
1	cup buttermilk
	Confectioner's sugar

Preheat oven to 350°.

Butter and flour a 10-inch tube pan or a bundt pan or two loaf tins.

Cream the butter and sugar together until fluffy. Add the eggs one at a time. Add the vanilla and lemon juice and blend well.

Sift together the flour, soda, baking powder and salt. Add the dry ingredients to the creamed mixture alternately with the buttermilk. Beat well after each addition. Batter should be smooth.

Pour into the prepared baking pan or tins. If using a tube or bundt pan, bake for one hour. If using the two loaf tins, bake 30–35 minutes.

Cool on a cake rack and unmold. Dust with confectioner's sugar. This cake freezes well.

Banana cake

	Butter for cake pan
¼	pound butter, at room temperature
1½	cups granulated sugar
3	large eggs, separated
1	rounded teaspoon baking soda
1	cup buttermilk or sour milk (see note)
¾	cup mashed ripe bananas
½	cup chopped nuts
2	cups flour
½	teaspoon baking powder
1	teaspoon vanilla

Preheat oven to 350°. Butter an 8- × 12-inch pan.

Cream the butter and sugar until light and fluffy. Blend in egg yolks. Stir baking soda into buttermilk and blend in. Blend in bananas and nuts.

Sift dry ingredients and add. Stir in vanilla. Beat egg whites until stiff and fold into mixture. Pour into the prepared pan and bake 50–60 minutes.

Note: If you have no buttermilk, sour regular milk by adding 1 tablespoon lemon juice to 1 cup room-temperature milk. Let stand 10 minutes until milk clabbers.

Walnut sponge cake

2	cups shelled walnuts
6	tablespoons flour
1	teaspoon cream of tartar
¼	teaspoon salt
10	medium eggs at room temperature, separated
1¼	cups sugar
1	teaspoon vanilla

Preheat oven to 375° for at least an hour.

Butter *bottom* only of a 10-inch angel food tube pan. Line the bottom with waxed paper cut to fit, and butter the paper. Finely grate nuts with a hand grater or in the food processor. Sift together the flour, cream of tartar, and salt and combine with nuts.

In a large bowl beat the eggs yolks with an electric beater, then gradually beat in sugar until mixture is thick. Stir in vanilla. Combine with flour mixture and blend well.

Beat the whites until stiff peaks form; stir about a third of them into the batter to lighten it, then gently fold in the remainder with a spatula. Pour into the prepared pan and bake in the lower third of the preheated oven 45–50 minutes or until a tester comes out clean.

Immediately invert the cake on a rack and let cool 1–1½ hours, then loosen sides with a spatula, remove pan, and carefully peel off paper. Serves 12.

Streusel Squares

COOKIE DOUGH:
½   pound butter, at room temperature
1   8-ounce package cream cheese
2   cups sifted all-purpose flour

Combine above ingredients and beat at slow speed with electric beater. Spread dough evenly in a 15- × 10- × 1-inch jelly roll pan.

CRUMB TOPPING:
14   tablespoons butter
3½   cups flour
1   teaspoon cinnamon
¾   cup light brown sugar
1   tablespoon vegetable oil
     Confectioner's sugar

Combine butter, flour, cinnamon, and sugar. Work together with hands. Add oil and continue working together until small uniform crumbs form. Sprinkle crumbs over batter and bake at 350° for 20 minutes.

Cool for 5 minutes, then cut into squares. Sprinkle generously with confectioner's sugar.

Note: Margarine may replace butter in this recipe.

Lemon squares

2   cups flour
1   cup butter or margarine at room temperature
½   cup confectioner's sugar
      Pinch salt
4   eggs, lightly beaten
2   cups sugar
4   tablespoons fresh lemon juice
1   teaspoon grated lemon rind
      Confectioner's sugar

Preheat oven to 350°.

Butter and flour a 9-inch square pan.

Mix the flour, butter, sugar, and salt together with a pastry blender until mixture resembles coarse meal. Pack into the prepared pan and bake 20 minutes. Remove from oven.

Mix the eggs, granulated sugar, lemon juice, and rind together, spread over cake and bake 25 minutes more. Cool for at least half an hour before cutting into squares. Sprinkle with confectioner's sugar. Makes 20–25 squares.

Ginger cookies

Use the recipe for Gingerbread men (see page 228), but roll dough about the thickness of a quarter. Use small cookie cutters, peel dough away from around shapes, re-roll scraps until all are used up. Makes about 4 dozen.

Fudge drop cookies

12	ounces semisweet chocolate bits
6	ounces butter or margarine
1	14-ounce can sweetened condensed milk
1	cup all-purpose flour, unsifted
1	teaspoon vanilla
1	cup chopped walnuts

Melt the chocolate and butter together in the top of a double boiler. Off heat, stir in the milk and blend in the flour. Stir in vanilla and nuts. Chill for at least 30 minutes.

Preheat oven to 350°. Drop by the teaspoonful onto a foil-lined baking sheet. Bake for 10–12 minutes. Cool thoroughly on wire racks. Makes about 65 cookies.

Gingerbread men

¼	cup butter
½	cup light brown sugar
½	cup dark molasses
3½	cups flour, sifted
1	teaspoon baking soda
¼	teaspoon ground cloves
½	teaspoon cinnamon
1	teaspoon ground ginger
½	teaspoon salt
¼	cup orange juice or water

Cream butter with sugar. Beat in molasses.

Sift together flour, soda, ground cloves, cinnamon, ginger, and salt. Add to butter mixture alternately with liquid, blending well after each addition. Form dough into a ball and chill for 30 minutes in refrigerator.

Preheat oven to 350°. Line 2 cookie sheets with foil and roll out dough thin (about ⅛ inch) on sheet. Cut desired shapes (classic gingerbread men, hearts, etc.). "Peel" away excess dough and reroll this on a second sheet. Make a small hole at the tops of cookies if they are to be hung. Bake 8–10 minutes or until lightly browned around edges. Cool on cookie sheet until firm, then remove with spatula.

Make facial features, clothing details, etc., with white icing piped through a tube. Makes ten 5-inch cookie men.

Soft molasses cookies

Ask any old-time Bonacker what food memories he has from childhood and chances are he will mention clam chowder and 'lasses cookies.

1¼	cups sugar
1	cup unsulfured molasses
1	cup melted lard (a must)
1	cup boiling water
2	tablespoons baking soda dissolved in ¼ cup water
2	eggs, lightly beaten
4½	cups flour
½	teaspoon salt
1	teaspoon cinnamon
1	teaspoon ground ginger
½	cup raisins (optional)

Preheat oven to 350°. Line cookie sheet with foil.

Mix together the sugar, molasses, shortening, and boiling water. Stir in baking soda mixture and eggs. Sift together flour, salt, and spices. Add to molasses mixture gradually, beating vigorously. Fold in raisins if used. Drop by teaspoonfuls onto prepared baking sheet. Bake 15–18 minutes. Makes about 5½ dozen 2"-diameter cookies.

Blueberry muffins

	Butter for muffin tins
2	cups flour
⅓	cup sugar
1	tablespoon baking powder
½	teaspoon salt
4	tablespoons butter, melted
1	cup milk
1	egg
	Flour
	Several gratings nutmeg
1	cup blueberries

Preheat oven to 425° and butter muffin tins.

Sift dry ingredients into a large bowl.

Break egg into a small bowl. Add melted butter to milk and stir both into egg. Pour over dry ingredients and beat briefly to blend. Shake a little flour over the berries to coat them, add a few gratings nutmeg, and fold gently into the batter.

Fill muffin cups ⅔ full and bake 20 minutes.

Makes 12 muffins.

Icebox bran muffins

The following recipe yields an enormous amount of muffins; the idea is to keep the unbaked mixture in the refrigerator (where it will keep, well covered, for up to one month) and bake as needed. If you don't wish to do this, halve all the ingredients.

4	cups Kellogg's All-Bran
2	cups Nabisco 100% Bran (see note)
½	cup dates, optional
1	cup raisins
2	cups boiling water
	Butter for muffin tins
1	cup shortening
2½	cups light brown sugar
4	eggs
1	quart buttermilk
5	cups flour
5	teaspoons baking soda
1	teaspoon salt

Mix the cereals, dates, and raisins with the boiling water and allow to cool.

Preheat oven to 400°. Butter or paper-line muffin tins.

Cream the sugar and shortening, stir in bran mixture, and blend well. Beat in the eggs, 1 at a time. Sift together flour, soda, and salt and add to bran mixture alternately with milk mixture, blending well after each addition.

Fill prepared tins ½ full and bake 20–25 minutes. Makes about 8 dozen.

Note: Nabisco 100% Bran is available in health food stores.

Pâté brisée

Success in handling this pastry is largely determined by working with a light, quick hand and using very cold butter and a chilled mixing bowl. A cool surface, such as marble, can also help the rolling out.

6   tablespoons butter, very cold, cut in tiny pieces
2   tablespoons vegetable shortening, chilled
1½   cups all-purpose flour
¼   teaspoon salt
3   tablespoons ice water

Combine butter, vegetable shortening, flour, and salt in a mixing bowl. Using fingertips or a pastry blender work quickly to blend the ingredients until mixture resembles cornmeal. Put 3 tablespoons of the ice water over the flour mixture and gather it together lightly into a ball. If dough does not adhere easily, add a few more drops of water as needed, but not more than a total of 2 additional tablespoons. Dust ball lightly with flour, flatten into a circle, wrap in plastic wrap or waxed paper, and refrigerate for at least 3 hours.

About 10 minutes before you plan to work with it, remove dough from refrigerator. Put on a floured surface, dust a bit of flour on top, and from the center, along the lines of spokes of a wheel, roll out a circle, lifting and turning dough as necessary. Sprinkle small amounts of additional flour on the board as needed. A baker's spatula may be helpful in lifting dough if it sticks to surface.

Using a plate of appropriate size, cut circles 1 inch larger than tartlet pans. Roll circle up over rolling pin and unroll over pan. Roll the pin hard over the pan rim to cut off excess (if using one large pan, do not cut circles but pick up entire piece of pastry on the pin and proceed as directed).

Prick bottom of pastry shell(s) and refrigerate 15–20 minutes.

Preheat oven to 400°.

While dough is chilling, cut circles of waxed paper in the same diameter as pan(s). Butter the circle(s) and fit over pastry. Drop raw beans or pie weights over paper. This will keep pastry from puffing up.

Bake 7–8 minutes, then remove pan(s) from oven, remove paper and beans or weights, prick pastry again and return to oven 7–10 minutes. When pastry starts to shrink in from sides and is lightly golden, remove from oven and cool on a wire rack.

This pastry may be used for any kind of fruit tarts and also in quiches. Pâté brisée shells may also be made ahead, carefully wrapped and frozen until needed.

Cream cheese pastry

4   ounces cream cheese
¼   pound unsalted butter
       Salt
1   cup flour

Put cream cheese and butter in a bowl with a pinch of salt and beat well to soften. Add flour slowly to blend well. Knead briefly and form into a ball. Wrap in waxed paper and chill in refrigerator until firm. This dough can also be frozen and used when needed.

Basic pie pastry

2½   cups sifted flour
1   teaspoon salt
¾   teaspoon baking powder
1   tablespoon sugar
12   tablespoons shortening (all Crisco or half butter, half Crisco)
5   tablespoons ice water

Sift the dry ingredients together; cut in shortening with a pastry blender or two knives, until mixture resembles small peas. Add ice water, 1 tablespoon at a time, using only enough to bind.

Chill dough in refrigerator at least one hour, then roll out on a lightly floured board to desired thickness. Yield: pastry for one 9-inch double-crust pie.

IN FOOD PROCESSOR:
Use the steel knife. Put all ingredients except water in bowl. Process a few seconds until mixture looks like small crumbs. Add water quickly through feeder tube, with motor on. When a clean ball of dough forms (20–50 seconds), remove, and chill as above.

EAST
Some Basic Sauces
HAMPTON

Mayonnaise

(blender)

1 egg and 1 egg yolk
5 teaspoons lemon juice
1 teaspoon dry mustard
1 teaspoon salt
¼ teaspoon white pepper
1 cup oil (can be ½ olive, ½ salad oil)

Whirl egg, lemon juice, mustard, salt, and pepper in a blender. Add oil in a slow, steady stream. Add 1 tablespoon warm water if it appears too thick. Makes about 1 cup.

Garlic mayonnaise

Press 2 or 3 cloves garlic into the blender jar after completing mayonnaise and blend briefly. Allow to "ripen" several hours before serving.

Horseradish mayonnaise

Blend in 2 tablespoons or more prepared horseradish to each cup of mayonnaise.

236　SOME BASIC SAUCES

Vinaigrette sauce, plain

2   tablespoons red wine vinegar
1   teaspoon salt
½   teaspoon Dijon-type mustard
        Freshly ground pepper
⅓   cup olive oil

Put vinegar in a small bowl. Add salt, mustard, pepper to taste, and beat with small whisk. Continue whisking while you add oil in slow steady stream. Makes about ½ cup dressing.

MUSTARD

Increase mustard in the above recipe to 2 teaspoons.

GARLIC

Crush a garlic clove with the side of a cleaver or the bottom of a skillet and let it steep in the dressing for a while.

LEMON

Substitute lemon juice for the vinegar in the basic vinaigrette dressing.

HERBED, FOR ARTICHOKES OR ASPARAGUS

Into a pint screw-top jar put:

1	tablespoon coarse salt
1	teaspoon freshly ground white pepper
½	teaspoon freshly ground black pepper
½	teaspoon sugar
½	teaspoon dry mustard
1	teaspoon Dijon mustard
1	teaspoon lemon juice
1	clove garlic, put through a press
5	tablespoons vinegar
2	tablespoons olive oil
10	tablespoons salad oil
1	egg
½	cup light cream

SHAKE, AND ADD:

1	finely chopped hard-cooked egg
1	tablespoon chopped parsley
1	tablespoon capers, drained

Sauce mousseline

Beat 2 egg whites until stiff peaks are formed. Fold into the above sauce.

Blender hollandaise

6 egg yolks
2 tablespoons ice water
½ pound sweet butter, melted and cooled
3 tablespoons lemon juice

Put yolks and water in the container of a blender. Blend briefly, add melted butter, then blend again.

Place mixture in a small heavy saucepan and cook over moderate heat 2–3 minutes, stirring. Pour back into blender jar, add lemon juice, blend again briefly. Yield: about 2 cups.

Cream sauce

(Bechamel sauce)

2 tablespoons butter
3 tablespoons flour
2 cups milk, hot
½ cup milk or heavy cream
  Salt and fresh white pepper
  Lemon juice

Melt butter over low heat. Blend in flour and cook, stirring constantly, 2–3 minutes until butter and flour bubble up but do not become brown.

Remove from heat and pour in the hot milk. Beat hard for 1 minute. Put sauce again over heat and cook, stirring, until it just comes to the boil. Let boil for a minute or two, still stirring. Lower heat and beat in milk or cream a little bit at a time. Season to taste with salt, pepper, and several drops of lemon juice.

Crème fraîche

This is a tangy but not sour-tasting cream that can be used in cooking in any recipe calling for sour cream, with the advantage that it will not curdle if boiled. It is delicious on fruits, especially berries.

1 tablespoon buttermilk
1 cup heavy cream

Combine buttermilk and cream and heat until lukewarm. Let stand in a warm place for about 6 hours or overnight, until thick. Stir, pour into a screw-top jar, and refrigerate. It will keep for 1½ to 2 weeks. Makes 1 cup.

Plain tomato sauce

3 tablespoons olive oil
1 large clove garlic, chopped
1 small onion, chopped
1 34-ounce can Italian tomatoes, drained and coarsely chopped
1 tablespoon chopped parsley
½ teaspoon salt
½ teaspoon freshly ground pepper
½ teaspoon oregano
1 tablespoon butter

Sauté garlic and onion in oil. Add tomatoes, parsley, salt, pepper, and oregano and butter, and simmer uncovered 15–20 minutes.

Correct seasoning if necessary. Makes about 4 cups.

Fresh tomato sauce for freezing

This is a recipe to have handy when your own vines suddenly yield more tomatoes than you can possibly eat or when you wish to take advantage of bargain-priced baskets of less than perfect tomatoes, which can be found at road-side stands or farmers' markets during peak harvest time. Remember that seasonings lose a lot of their strength in the freezer, so plan to taste and season again when you defrost.

The sauce can subsequently be used for pasta, for vegetables, to make soup, or, after straining, in any recipe calling for tomato sauce.

4	tablespoons butter
4	tablespoons olive oil
5	cups chopped onions
10	cloves garlic, minced
4	quarts chopped tomatoes, measured after juicing (see note)
	Salt, freshly ground black pepper
½	cup chopped basil leaves or 10 sprigs fresh thyme or 5 teaspoons dried thyme

Melt butter in olive oil in a large deep enamel-on-cast-iron or stainless steel pot (you may have to use two). Sauté onions and garlic until transparent.

Add tomatoes by handfuls, giving them a last squeeze as you do to divest them of more juice. Add seasonings and cook 15 minutes. Put through a food mill. Ladle into plastic containers when cool. Yields about 5 quarts.

Note: Preparing the tomatoes: As tomatoes contain a lot of water, a richer sauce can be obtained if they are ''juiced'' first. Remove stem end and cut tomato in half, vertically. Squeeze each half slightly over the sink. Let the squeezed halves sit in a bowl for 15 minutes or so and then drain them in a large colander.

Pesto

(a sauce for pasta)

2	cups basil leaves, tightly packed
½	cup olive oil
¼	cup pine nuts (pignoli)
2–3	cloves garlic
½	cup chopped parsley, preferably Italian
	Salt, freshly ground pepper
½	cup grated Parmesan cheese
½	cup grated Romano cheese
2	tablespoons softened butter

Put basil leaves in food processor, add olive oil, pine nuts, garlic, parsley, and salt and pepper to taste, and blend. Add cheeses and butter and blend into a smooth paste.

Warm a large pottery bowl while pasta is cooking. Put pesto in bowl. When pasta is done, fork it directly into the warmed bowl. Toss with the sauce. Add 3 to 4 tablespoons of the hot pasta water and toss again. Makes enough sauce for 1 pound of pasta. Serves 4–6.

Note: Leftover pesto sauce can be refrigerated well for a week. It also freezes well. If making pesto exclusively for the freezer, omit the cheese and butter and stir these ingredients in after defrosting.

Crème anglaise

(custard sauce)

8	egg yolks
⅔–1	cup granulated sugar (depending on desired sweetness)
2	cups light cream
3	tablespoons brandy or 2 teaspoons vanilla

242   SOME BASIC SAUCES

Beat egg yolks until slightly thickened; add sugar and continue beating until mixture forms a ribbon. Heat cream to scalding and add in droplets, beating constantly.

Cook in the top of a double boiler or in a heavy pot over direct heat, stirring constantly until mixture is thickened and coats the spoon.

Immediately remove from heat. When slightly cooled, stir in brandy or vanilla, strain, and chill.

Note: This recipe may be halved. If made with brandy, the sauce will keep for at least a week in the refrigerator in a screw-top jar. A less rich version can be obtained by using milk instead of cream.

Some Useful Hints...

Ginger root can be kept indefinitely if peeled and immersed in sherry in a screw-top jar.

Egg whites can be stored in the freezer, defrosted so the needed amount may be removed and the balance refrozen. One-quarter cup of egg whites equals 2 whites.

Egg whites—beating: Egg whites to be folded into a soufflé or mousse are properly beaten when the bowl can be turned upside down and they do not begin to slide out.

Seasoning a skillet: There is less chance of foods, especially omelets, sticking in a well-seasoned skillet. (New skillets should be seasoned before use, as well as one that has not been used for a long time.) Clean pan, if it is new, and dry thoroughly. Put in about ½-inch salad oil and heat very slowly on top of stove or in a slow oven until oil is very hot. Let pan cool with oil in it, discard oil, and wipe out with a paper towel.

To thoroughly dissolve (clarify) gelatin:
Soften 1 envelope in ¼ cup cold water in a Pyrex measuring cup or pudding dish. Fill a small skillet with 2 inches of water. Put the Pyrex cup in the skillet, and bring the water to a boil. Simmer until ready to use, stirring gelatin occasionally with a wooden spoon. When it becomes almost clear in color, it is dissolved.

When baking a "blind" pastry shell (without filling) put a couple handfuls of rice or beans or pie weights on a waxed-paper round laid on the dough, to keep pastry from bubbling.

From an East Hampton cookbook of 1848: "A roasted onion, bound on the wrist over the pulse, will relieve the most inveterate toothache in a few moments."

To make whipping heavy cream easier, chill bowl and beaters first.

To vary the flavor of meat done on the charcoal grill, throw a handful of a fragrant herb (rosemary, thyme, sage, bay leaves) on coals for the last couple minutes of cooking.

When charcoal-broiling a whole fish in a wire fish grill, heat the grill first, and flour and oil the fish well before insertion.

Contributors

Mrs. David Abrahamsen	Mr. Bert Greene
Mrs. Richard P. Adams	Mr. Robert Gruen
Mrs. John T. Allen	Mrs. Steven Hahn
Mrs. David C. Baker, Jr.	Mrs. Crawford C. Halsey
Mrs. Edward M. Baker, Jr.	Mrs. Richard Hammerman
Mr. James Beard	Mrs. George B. Hand
Mrs. K. E. Benzenberg	Mrs. Claus Hoie
Mrs. Raymond Bigar	Mr. Hugh Horner
Mrs. W. Earle Blackburn	Mrs. Jane Huggins
Mrs. W. Conant Brewer	Mrs. Sal Iacono
Mrs. Giraud Chester	Mrs. Frank Jewels
Mrs. Fanny Crawford	Mrs. Edward H. Jewett, Jr.
Mrs. Joan Straus Cullman	Mrs. Oswald Jones
Mrs. Annie Damaz	Mrs. Jacob Kaplan
Mrs. Dierdre David	Mrs. E. Coe Kerr, Jr.
Mrs. Frank Dayton	Mrs. Edward Kilroe
Mrs. Sherrill Dayton	Mrs. Alexander M. Laughlin
Mrs. Alfred Devendorf	Mr. Hubert Long
Mrs. Robert C. Duncan	Mrs. Shary Lowndes
Mrs. Lee Eastman	Mrs. Frank Loy
Mrs. Meg Eberhart	Mrs. Rachel Lugassy
Mrs. Louis T. Edwards	Mrs. Martin Lukashok
Mr. John Eyre	Mrs. John K. Lundberg
Mrs. Susan Eyre	Mrs. Robert W. Lynch, Jr.
Mrs. Florence Fabricant	Mrs. Edward I. Martin
Mrs. Kimberly Farkas	Mrs. James T. McGuirk
Mrs. Herbert French	Mrs. Raymond Medlar
Mrs. Donald Gordon	Mrs. Robert Mulford

Mr. Hans Namuth

Mrs. Cassard O'Brien

Miss Catherine O'Brien

Miss Edwardina O'Brien

Mrs. Donald Pels

Mrs. Charles R. Potter

Mrs. Ruby Price

Mrs. Federico Quadrani

Mrs. Robert Schmidt

Mrs. Kyrle Simond

Mrs. Arthur Smith

Mrs. Alfred Spear

Mrs. Frederick Spencer

Mrs. Gladys Stewart

Miss Beverly Taylor

Mrs. Frank Tercy

Mrs. Peter Terian

Mrs. Douglas Thomas

Mr. Maurice Thorens

Mrs. Daniel Tucker

Mr. P. V. Vitaldhas

Mrs. Parsons Wainwright

Mrs. Wings White

Mrs. Elwood Whitney

Mrs. Harry L. Willard

Mrs. Jon Wurtzburger

Mrs. Jeanette Young

EAST

Index

HAMPTON

Index

A

acorn squash, baked, 175
almond crescent cookies, 85
Alsatian cabbage and potatoes, 91
applecake with whipped cream, 92
apple crisp, 88
apple pie, 46
apples, baked, 17
applesauce, 144
apple soup, cold curried, 113
apricot mousse, 53
apricot squares, 166
Arborio rice, 49, 93
Armenian rice pilaff with noodles, 84
artichokes vinaigrette, 82
    sauce for, 238
asparagus, 104
    sauces for, 238
asparagus salad, hot, 25
August blackberry pie, 132

B

bacon, oven-baked, 7

bacon-broiled clams, 191
banana cake, 224
banana-orange muffins, 218
bananas baked with rum, 82
barbecue
    chicken, 120
    holiday, 124
    leg of lamb, 126
basic pie pastry, 234
basil
    sauce, *see* pesto
    tomato salad with, 29
bass, *see* sea bass; striped bass
beach plum jelly, 206–7
beach plum pie, 36
beach plum pudding, 24
beans
    green, with mushrooms, 175
    green, vinaigrette, 114
    white pea, baked, 66
bean salad, 40
Beard, James, steak sandwich recipe of, 199
beef
    cauliflower, snow peas, and, 81